Day Hiker's Guide
to
Vermont

1989

Third Edition

Second Printing

$7.50

Published by

THE GREEN MOUNTAIN CLUB, INC.
POST OFFICE BOX 889
MONTPELIER, VERMONT 05602

Printed By
Northlight Studio Press, Inc.
Barre, Vermont

ISBN   0-318-12119-0

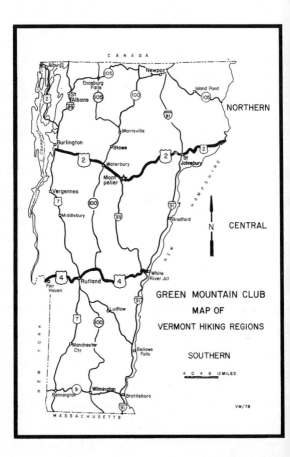

GREEN MOUNTAIN CLUB

MAP OF

VERMONT HIKING REGIONS

SOUTHERN

4 0 4 8 12 MILES

VM/78

DEDICATION

MINERVA HINCHEY
1895-1979

This third edition of the *Day Hiker's Guide to Vermont* is dedicated to Miss Minerva Hinchey, a long-time member of the Green Mountain Club, who died on March 26, 1979.

Minerva's long and important role in the history of the GMC began in 1955. In that year she joined the Killington Section of the GMC, and acted as the Club's corresponding secretary and business manager of *The Long Trail News* in her spare time.

In the ensuing years the amount of GMC correspondence grew to the point where the Club's Board of Trustees voted Minerva a yearly salary of $250.00. This made her the Club's first paid employee with the exception of the summer trail crews.

For 22 years Minerva served the Club in these two roles. She felt the most enjoyable part of her job was meeting GMC members and other hikers who visited the office. In early 1977 she retired as secretary and business manager but stayed on as part time bookkeeper. Later that year she began full retirement.

Minerva will long be remembered by her friends and the many hikers she helped in those 22 years.

TABLE OF CONTENTS

PREFACE

We hope this new edition of the *Day Hiker's Guide to Vermont* will answer many questions asked by visitors and residents regarding hiking opportunities in the state. In addition to descriptions of approximately 150 trails, the book provides general information on equipment, proper hiking practices, and trail management. With few exceptions, these trails are not part of the Long Trail System, and are not maintained by the Green Mountain Club. We have attempted to provide current information on the hikes included, but trail changes can occur on short notice.

Those familiar with previous editions of this guide will note some changes. Most noticeable is the reorganization of the text into three geographic regions. Readers may also notice that several trails included in prior editions have been eliminated. We decided to remove trails that are difficult or impossible to follow due to lack of maintenance, logging activity, or other development.

Many people have contributed to this project over the last two years. Unfortunately, it isn't possible to recognize them all here, but several deserve special recognition.

Our thanks to Cleo Billings for her excellent sketches and new cover design.

We appreciate the cartography originally done in 1978 by University of Vermont students working under the direction of Professor H. Gardiner Barnum. For this edition, many of these maps have been redrawn in color, others have been revised, and new maps have been added. All this work was performed by Middlebury College geography student Theresa McCoy. Theresa worked with Professor Robert Churchill on this project. We thank them both for this major contribution.

We thank the many GMC members who spent countless hours in the field checking trail descriptions. Kathy Astrauckas, Clare and Michael Fishbach, Michele Fitzgerald, John Lepinski, Dave Morse, Jeanne Sicard, Earl and Edna Williams, and Philip Woodbury were the major contributors to this effort.

The staffs of the Vermont Agency of Environmental Conservation and U.S. Forest Service provided current information on trails located on public land. Bill Guenther, Gary Sabourin, Gary Salmon, and Steve Sinclair of the Vermont Department of Forests, Parks and Recreation, and Russ Eastwood of the Green Mountain National Forest were particularly helpful.

This new edition would never have gone to press without the assistance of the GMC staff. Mary Deaett, the Club's Executive Assistant, handled many important details. Field Assistants Ray Auger and Ben Davis checked trails, and provided many helpful suggestions on the text. Executive Director Harry T. Peet, Jr. provided much needed guidance from the beginning.

Our heartfelt thanks to everyone who contributed in some way to the publication of this guide book.

Brian T. Fitzgerald
Robert P. Lindemann, *Editors*

INTRODUCTION

The primary purpose of this guide is to describe many of the short trails suitable for day hiking that are scattered about Vermont. These trails encompass a wide range of purpose, length, difficulty, and other important characteristics. Because of this diversity, we recommend that prospective hikers read the introductory material as well as the individual hike descriptions before heading into the field. Hikers should also keep in mind that trail changes can occur at any time. If possible, obtain up to date information prior to your hike.

For the most part, the trails described here are not part of the Long Trail System, as described in the Green Mountain Club's *Guide Book of the Long Trail*. Most of the trails described are hiking trails on public and private land, but there are also public "multi-use" trails, nature trails and some abandoned or country roads. All of the trail descriptions are based on recent field checks or other reliable information.

This volume certainly does not include every Vermont hiking trail that is not part of the Long Trail System. In some cases this was intentional, either because a trail is poorly or irregularly maintained, or due to logging or other activities that have temporarily disrupted the trail. In other instances, we simply are unaware of a particular trail's existence. We hope that readers of this book will contact the Green Mountain Club if they have any information that should be included in future editions.

THE GREEN MOUNTAIN CLUB

Historical Highlights

On March 11, 1910, twenty-three prominent Vermonters met in Burlington and founded the Green Mountain Club "to make the Vermont mountains play a larger part in the life of the people." James P. Taylor, Associate Headmaster at Vermont Academy in Saxton's River, was the driving force behind the new organization. It was he who first became disenchanted with the lack of hiking trails in the Green Mountains, and set out to do something about it.

The Club's first major objective, unprecedented in concept and magnitude, was to fulfill Taylor's cherished dream of a Long Trail, a continuous footpath which would follow the length of the Green Mountains from Massachusetts to Canada. Gradually the formidable difficulties of scouting and cutting a trail through long stretches of nearly impenetrable ridgeline wilderness were overcome, and in 1930 the final link from a temporary terminus on Jay Peak to Milepost 592 on the Quebec border was completed.

Well before the Long Trail was completed, the Club had made progress in several other areas. Members organized several Sections (local chapters), both within and outside of Vermont, to maintain and improve the trail system. Section members and other volunteers rerouted much of the Long Trail to more scenic ridgeline locations. Many side trails were built to provide easier access to popular areas, and work was begun on a system of shelters to provide overnight accommodations for hikers. In 1917, the GMC published the first edition of the *Guide Book of the Long Trail*.

The year after the final segment of the trail was completed, the Club established its salaried trail crew, the Long Trail Patrol. Since then, the LTP has spent summers assisting the volunteer members and friends of the Green Mountain Club with trail and shelter maintenance and construction. For its first thirty-six years, the Patrol was led by its founder, the late Professor Roy O. Buchanan of the University of Vermont.

In the early 1970's, the Club recognized that the popularity of the Trail and the resulting overuse posed a threat to the integrity of the LT. As a result, the Club adopted stricter standards for trail and shelter maintenance, redirected the Long Trail Patrol to concentrate on heavy trail construction, and expanded the Caretaker and Ranger-Naturalist programs to provide more hiker education in the field. The GMC also entered into formal agreements with the State of Vermont and U.S. Forest Service, which share with the Club the responsibility for management, maintenance, and improvement of the Long Trail System.

Fortunately, use of the Long Trail leveled off in the late 1970's and has remained fairly steady since then. More recently, however, the threat of development has posed a new challenge to the GMC. Approximately 30% of the LT crosses private land, and much of this land is either being developed or is up for sale. The Club is now beginning a major land protection effort to ensure that the integrity of the Long Trail will be maintained.

In 1971 the Vermont legislature recognized the Green Mountain Club as the "founder, sponsor, defender and protector of the Long Trail system" and further charged the Club with responsibility for developing policies and coordinating efforts concerned with the "preservation, maintenance and proper use" of hiking trails in Vermont.

In 1985 the General Assembly reaffirmed this trust with another resolution. The legislators noted that the Green Mountain Club was celebrating its 75th anniversary and that the Long Trail "is both an inspiration and a source of enjoyment for the people of Vermont and her visitors." The lawmakers backed the GMC's trail protection activities by endorsing the "voluntary transfer of perpetual rights-of-way by private property owners to the Green Mountain Club, private land trusts, and public agencies", and encouraged "federal, state and local cooperation in this effort to preserve the continuity and scenic qualities of the Long Trail and its side trails."

Membership

Membership in the Green Mountain Club is the hiker's way of supporting hiking in Vermont, and is open to anyone with an interest in the Green Mountains. Two types of membership are available: those wishing to participate directly in trail maintenance, outings, and other functions may join one of the Sections, or local chapters. Those who desire to support the work of the Club, but are not interested in joining a Section may become an At-Large member. Of the Clubs 5,000 members, 55% are members-at-large.

Both Section and At-Large members enjoy the same benefits: membership card, subscription to *The Long Trail News*, the Club's quarterly periodical, discounts on Club publications, and reduced use fees at some locations served by GMC caretakers.

There are presently fourteen GMC Sections. Ten are based in Vermont: Bennington, Brattleboro, Killington, (Rutland area), Bread Loaf (Middlebury area), Burlington, Laraway (Northwestern Vermont), Manchester, Montpelier, Ottauquechee (Woodstock area), and Sterling (Morrisville area). Four are based out-of-state: New York (NYC area), Connecticut (Hartford area), Worcester, Mass., and Pioneer Valley (Springfield, Mass. area). Each Section is responsible for the maintenance of a designated stretch of the Long Trail. The Sections are largely autonomous, and each has its own organizational structure.

Section and At-Large membership is available to anyone simply by submitting the application in the back of this guide book with a check for the appropriate dues amount.

Publications and Services

Besides the *Day Hiker's Guide to Vermont* and *The Long Trail News*, the GMC publishes the *Guide Book of the Long Trail*, now in its twenty-third edition. A number of maps and pamphlets are also available. The Club also offers two slide shows with taped narration. The various publications and slide shows are described in the Appendix of this guide book. The Club office also stocks a number of Forest Service and State information leaflets.

The GMC staff will gladly respond to telephone or written inquiries dealing with hiking in Vermont. If your question cannot be answered by reading this guide book contact the Club office.

Organizational Structure

The Green Mountain Club is a non-profit organization governed by its Board of Directors, which represents Sections, At-Large members, the U.S. Forest Service, and Vermont Department of Forests, Parks, and Recreation. A list of current officers and directors is published each August in *The Long Trail News*.

The Club holds its Annual Meeting on the Saturday nearest Memorial Day. The business meeting is only a part of this spring get-together which includes informal talks, camping, hikes, and work parties. Another gathering of GMC'ers is the Intersectional, which is held at the end of

August. This week-long event takes place at a base camp near the Long Trail, and features daily hikes, family camping, and evening programs. Guests are always welcome.

A MEANINGFUL CONTRIBUTION

The Green Mountain Club depends upon many people donating time and energy to maintain and protect The Long Trail - America's oldest long distance hiking trail. Their efforts have been strengthened immeasurably by thousands of people who provide valuable financial support to the Club. Currently, the Club is in need of new contributors.

YOU CAN HELP US TO
- protect and preserve the Trail
- maintain and reconstruct the Trail
- educate and inform the public
- sustain the quality of Vermont's unique environment

Contributions can be made today by sending a tax-deductible check to the address indicated below.

Some prefer to include the Club in their future financial plans. Bequests under wills have served to establish the Club's endowment fund - the income is used to meet a portion of the Club's operating budget. Bequests can take the form of cash, designated securities, other property or a portion of one's estate. We can help you plan.

For more information on estate planning and annual giving please write: THE GREEN MOUNTAIN CLUB, INC., P.O. Box 889, Montpelier, VT. 05602 or call (802) 223-3463

AN ACCOMPLISHMENT OF LASTING VALUE

VERMONT HIKING TRAILS

The Long Trail

Known for many years as the "Footpath in the Wilderness," the Long Trail follows the Green Mountains for about 265 miles from the Massachusetts line to the Canadian border. Although basically a ridgeline route which passes over more than forty of the state's highest peaks, the trail often descends to lower elevations to follow streams, skirt ponds, or pass through other areas of esthetic or historical interest. Included in the Long Trail System are a number of side and approach trails, totaling about 175 miles, and about 70 simple overnight shelters and primitive tent camping areas.

In conjunction with the numerous highway crossings and the many approach trails, the Long Trail offers many opportunities for day hiking. However, many longer or less accessible sections are best enjoyed by well prepared and properly equipped hikers willing to spend one or more nights on the trail. Whether day hikes or more ambitious trips are involved, however, the hiker should have the current edition of the *Guide Book of the Long Trail* and be familiar with the rules and courtesies governing responsible use of the trails and shelters.

The Appalachian Trail

Following a 2100 mile route from Maine to Georgia, the Appalachian Trail was first proposed by the late Benton MacKaye in 1921 and eventually completed in 1937. Like the Long Trail, which served as its model, the Appalachian Trail has since undergone numerous relocations to enhance its wilderness character.

In Vermont the Appalachian Trail follows the Long Trail from the Massachusetts state line to a point north of Sherburne Pass, east of Rutland. There it turns to the east and follows its own route for forty miles across the state to the Connecticut River at Hanover, N.H. The GMC maintains the section of the Appalachian Trail between Sherburne Pass and Vt. 12, while the Dartmouth Outing Club maintains the trail east from Vt. 12 and into New Hampshire. Access to the Appalachian Trail is limited to the north-south highway crossings in this area, and overnight camping facilities are limited.

The Appalachian Trail Conference, of which the Green Mountain Club is a member, publishes a detailed *Guide to the Appalachian Trail in New Hampshire and Vermont* and various other publications concerning the Appalachian Trail.

Other Hiking Trails

A variety of established foot trails, unrelated to the Long Trail system, are scattered throughout the state on private, state, and federal lands. A number of trails on private property are of obscure origin and manage to remain in existence despite lack of maintenance by individuals or organizations. Elsewhere, organizations such as the Ascutney Trails Association, the Taconic Hiking Club, the Westmore Association, and various summer camps have been active in restoring abandoned trails and constructing new routes. Many of these privately maintained trails are described in this guide, but coverage is by no means complete.

Many of the established trails on Green Mountain National Forest lands are directly or indirectly associated with the Long Trail. Most of the other widely dispersed trails are described in this book. Some trails that lie within designated Wilderness are more primitive than those elsewhere, so hikers should take special care to avoid losing their way.

A large number of trails are maintained within the various state forests and parks by the Vermont Department of Forests, Parks and Recreation. Most are individual trails or loops ranging from a half mile to three miles in length. In some of the older and larger areas, however, extensive networks have been developed. Most of the trails on state lands are described in this guide; in addition, trail maps are available in many of the state parks.

Multiuse Trails

In recent years, the Vermont Department of Forests, Parks and Recreation has established many miles of multiuse trails on state lands. Although primarily intended for snowmobiling and in part financed with money from snowmobile registrations, these trails are open to all nonmotorized recreational use in season. In general, these trails follow old woods roads and abandoned or unmaintained town roads. For the most part, they are well suited for day hik-

ing, but some tend to be obscured in places by berry bushes
and other lush summer growth. This guide provides information about some of these multiuse trails, but no attempt is made to describe their extensions across private
lands, where they are maintained by private snowmobile
clubs.

Nature Trails

Although perhaps of marginal interest to more experienced hikers looking for more demanding routes, the
various nature trails maintained by private organizations
and public agencies merit some attention in this guide.
However, the listing is far from complete, and local inquiry
no doubt will reveal the existence of many other nature
trails.

Aside from their obvious educational value and the
fascinating insights which they can provide, a number of
these nature trails are sufficiently long and varied in interest to meet the needs of nonhikers, novices, families with
small children, and others with limited hiking interests.
Nearly all of the trails are self-guiding, and opportunities
are usually available to borrow or purchase trail guides.
Several of the state parks and a few of the private organizations provide resident naturalists, nature museums, and
various field programs in addition to the nature trails.

Fire Tower Trails

Vermont's once extensive network of fire towers was
discontinued about 1973. Since then a number of them,
especially those on leased private property, have been
dismantled, more often than not resulting in the loss of
views from the heavily wooded summits. With very few
exceptions, the remaining towers are no longer maintained. In view of their abandoned status and probable
deterioration, hikers should make minimal use of these
towers, employ extreme caution when doing so, and clearly
recognize that they use them at their own risk.

Many of the abandoned fire tower routes are rapidly
becoming obscure, and only reasonably experienced and
observant hikers should attempt to follow them. While a
few such trails are described in this book, the primary reason
for doing so is to update previously published information
which may still be in general circulation.

Ski Touring Trails

Except for mention of coinciding or intersecting trails, no attempt is made to describe the rapidly growing number of ski touring trails. However, some basic reference sources are listed in the Appendix, and additional information can be obtained, from ski areas, touring centers, and ski shops.

TRAIL ACCESS AND HIKING BASES

The regional maps used in this book are intended only to show the general location of trails with respect to major highways and communities. For general travel purposes the *Vermont Official State Map and Touring Guide* is extremely useful. The map is available without charge at the numerous local information centers or by mail from the Vermont Travel Division, 134 State St., Montpelier, Vt. 05602. Another useful resource is *The Vermont Road Atlas and Guide* by Northern Cartographic (P.O. Box 133, Burlington, Vt. 05402). The atlas is available in most local bookstores.

Many of the trails described in this guide are reasonably accessible by Vermont Transit Lines buses, which operate with varying frequency over many of the major highways. Current timetables, which also show the schedules of connecting carriers, can be obtained at most bus depots in the Northeast or from Vermont Transit Lines, 135 St. Paul St., Burlington, Vt. 05401 (Telephone 802-864-6811). Taxi service is available in most of the larger communities.

Generally, overnight camping is not available along the trails described in this book, and prospective overnight campers should plan to use nearby public or private campgrounds. Most of the public and private campgrounds are listed on the reverse side of the *Vermont Official State Map and Touring Guide*. Additional information can be obtained from the Forest Supervisor, Green Mountain National Forest, P.O. Box 519, Rutland, Vt. 05701 and from the Vermont Department of Forests, Parks, and Recreation, 103 South Main St., Waterbury, VT 05676. Additional information about private campgrounds is available from the Vermont Travel Division at the above address.

Before using many of the state park trails, it may be necessary to pay the standard day-use entrance fee. Current fees are one dollar per adult for areas located on bodies of water and seventy-five cents per adult for other areas. Parking arrangements should be made with the park manager.

CLOTHING AND EQUIPMENT

Because most Vermont trails are rough underfoot and have many wet and muddy places, it is essential to wear sturdy, well broken-in footgear with adequate ankle support, heavy soles, and reasonable resistance to moisture. More often than not, street shoes and other casual footwear are not only inadequate and easily ruined but potentially hazardous. Until a long-term investment in expensive hiking boots can be justified, good quality work boots, six to ten inches high, with slip-resistant rubber soles are usually adequate for general hiking use. Unless the manufacturer provides different instructions, boots should be treated from time to time with silicone or other water repellent preparations.

Wear at least one pair of medium weight wool socks. Besides providing more insulation and cushioning, the wicking effect of wool helps to remove excess perspiration and other incidental moisture from the boots.

Outerwear should be durable, comfortable, and loose fitting without being floppy enough to catch on the brush and snags often encountered. Material with a fairly open weave which allows "breathing" is usually more comfortable than tightly woven fabrics. Although often overlooked, a comfortable hat with a broad brim or visor protects the head from heat and the eyes from glare.

Hiking shorts are often appropriate, but an extra pair of long pants is welcome insurance against sudden temperature drops, black flies, nettles, and berry bushes. A heavy shirt or windproof jacket provides protection against the cooler temperatures and brisk winds often encountered at higher elevations, while a rainsuit or poncho offers protection from sudden showers.

A day pack, available in many styles and sizes, is useful for longer trips. In addition to the extra clothing mentioned, provide room for a trail lunch, canteen or water bottle, guide book or trail maps, basic first aid kit, matches in a waterproof container, sturdy pocket knife, and a flashlight. Carry one or more small plastic bags for such things as storing wet clothing or transporting luncheon refuse and trail litter to a proper disposal site.

Optional items include a camera with extra film, sun glasses, insect repellent in non-aerosol form, toilet paper, and a small notebook and pencil for taking field notes or recording easily forgotten data about photographs.

USING THE TRAILS

Provided reasonable care and alertness as exercised, most of the trails described in this book can be used with confidence by relatively inexperienced hikers. Before using any of the trails, however, the hiker should carefully study the information provided and determine whether a proposed trip is suitable given his or her experience and capabilities. Beginners should first gain some experience on the shorter and easier trails before attempting longer and more demanding hikes.

The hiker should realize that markings and general trail conditions often leave much to be desired, but a well defined trailbed and indications of past clearing and blowdown removal will usually be apparent to an observant traveler. A few trails have been neglected for so long that routing is obscure and difficult to follow. They should be used only by reasonably experienced hikers accustomed to route finding.

Trail Marking

The Long Trail and Appalachian Trail are marked with rectangular white-painted blazes, and their associated side trails are usually marked with similar blue blazes. These blazes may be supplemented with arrows or signs.

On state and National Forest lands, most hiking trails are marked with blue-painted blazes. Multi-use trails on state lands are usually marked with orange diamonds, sometimes supplemented with blue paint blazes. Privately maintained trails are marked in various ways. Property lines which intersect or parallel many trails are painted in various colors, but the distinctly different manner in which boundary blazes are placed and the absence of a well defined pathway usually minimize the possibility of confusion.

Should the next blaze or other clear indication of the trail not be found within a reasonable distance, the hiker should **stop, look around** very carefully, and **backtrack** if necessary. A few minutes spent looking for the correct route as soon as uncertainty arises can avoid many hours of anxiety and embarrassment which often result from forging ahead too far on the wrong route.

Trail Courtesy

Hikers should treat the private and public lands they use with the same care and appreciation as their own prized property. By following these few common sense rules of courtesy conflicts with landowners and other hikers can be avoided.

When parking at trailheads, use parking areas or roadside turnouts if possible. Take care not to obstruct traffic or block access to homes and farms. Be sure to check with the landowner before parking on private property. Avoid damaging fences, and leave all gates and barways the way you found them.

Carry out all trash, including the litter left behind by less considerate hikers, for proper disposal. Bury human wastes well away from trails and water sources. Don't establish any new or relocated trails, fireplaces, or campsites without first obtaining permission.

Many wildflowers are protected by state law, so leave them undisturbed for others to enjoy.

Pets are best left at home, but if you bring an animal into the woods be sure to keep it under control at all times.

Fires and Overnight Camping

With very few exceptions, authorized fireplaces and campsites are not provided along the trails described in this guide, and prospective overnight hikers should usually plan to stay at nearby private or public campgrounds.

Under Vermont laws, it is necessary to obtain permission from the landowner or his agent before camping overnight at any time on private property or before building a fire on private land between April 1 and November 1. In the few places where formally maintained sites have been allowed by cooperating landowners, it is usually safe to assume that permission already has been granted to camp or to use the official fireplaces provided. Usually, however, fires and camping have been prohibited by the landowners, and failure to respect these reasonable restrictions could possibly result in the closure of many trails on private property.

Fires and overnight camping on lands controlled by the State of Vermont or the numerous local governments are restricted by law to those sites designated by the administering authorities. Camping on state lands is permitted only at specific sites in developed campgrounds, and below 2500 ft. elevation under the State's Primitive Camping Guidelines. Fires are restricted to the fireplaces and charcoal grilles provided at designated picnic areas and campsites. For information on Primitive Camping on State lands, contact the Department of Forests, Parks, and Recreation.

On Green Mountain National Forest lands, hikers are expected to follow strict fire safety procedures and to observe accepted "no trace" camping practices. Certain restrictions pertaining to fires and camping remain in effect at designated National Forest recreation areas. These regulations are prominently posted adjacent to those areas.

Water Supplies

The reliability and safety of trailside water sources should not be taken for granted. Especially at higher elevations, the certainty of finding water at locations mentioned in the guide varies from season to season in response to long-term weather conditions and other factors.

Even in remote areas, pollution of water supplies can be a problem. To be on the safe side, carry water from a source known to be safe. Boil, treat, or filter all water obtained in the field before drinking. Giardia is the most common illness that results from drinking polluted water, and results in severe discomfort and dehydration. This infection has not been a major problem in Vermont, but it is being reported with increasing frequency. Hikers should exercise caution to avoid being stricken.

Winter and Early Spring Use

Many trails are well suited for travel on snowshoes or skis provided the limitations and problems of winter use are recognized. In general, winter trips should be undertaken only by properly equipped groups, under experienced leaders, and over familiar trails which will not overtax the ability or experience of any member.

Winter trips typically take two to three times as long to complete as summer hikes, and the shorter periods of daylight and the fact that many access roads are unplowed are also limiting factors in trip planning. In general, trails at higher elevations are so obliterated by deep and drifted snow that the excessive expenditures of time and energy involved in route finding cannot be justified. Regardless of elevation, abrupt changes in weather conditions and the effects of the "wind chill factor" pose definite hazards to the unwary and unprepared winter traveler.

Depending on elevation and exposure, many trails are not reasonably free of snow until late April, and higher elevation routes are often snowbound until late May or early June. Aside from the fact that severe winter conditions can still be encountered, spring hiking in deep and rotten snow tends to be tiring and extremely arduous. In addition, the spring runoff makes many trails very wet and muddy, at which time they are very vulnerable to erosion and other permanent damage from hiker's boots. The GMC recommends hikers restrict their spring hiking to firm and dry trails at lower elevations until late May.

USING THE GUIDE BOOK

For guide book purposes, the state has been divided into three Regions, the limits of which are shown on the map on page 2. The individual Region maps preceding the descriptions are intended only to show the approximate location of trails with respect to principal towns and major highways. Detailed instructions for reaching those trails from well defined reference points are included in each trail description.

The various maps accompanying the descriptions are based on standard USGS topographic maps, which are identified in the text. Because of wide variations in area coverage, scale is not consistent from map to map. Foot trails are shown as heavy dashes, multi-use trails as dots, and other trails, usually identified in the text, as alternating dots and dashes. In some cases, trail classification and trail nomenclature are arbitrarily assigned.

Broken lines are used to distinguish roads which may not be passable in season from those which usually are. The demarcation is indefinite, as are the actual beginnings of the various trails. Road designation does not apply during winter, when many back roads are not plowed, or during the spring mud season.

Although route descriptions are provided in varying amounts of detail to reflect trail conditions or to note features which may merit further attention from the hiker, no attempt is made to provide step by step descriptions. That is the function of the signs, blazes, and other trail markings discussed under USING THE TRAILS. In some cases, mileage given in the concluding summary may be somewhat greater than stated in the route description, the difference usually being the additional distance required to reach the trail via connecting trail or road from a parking area or other normal point of beginning.

Trail mileages are cumulative from the trailhead or junction. Decimal figures, rounded to the nearest tenth of a mile, are used for known distances obtained with a measuring wheel, and fractional figures are used for estimated distances. Very short distances, whether measured or estimated, are given in feet.

Hiking times given in the text are based on the commonly used formula which assumes a half hour per mile plus an additional half hour for each thousand feet of climbing. These figures are for actual hiking only, and additional time should be allowed for resting, lunching, enjoying the views, and other satisfying pauses and delays en route. By themselves, guide book times have little meaning. With experience, however, each individual should discover a reasonably consistent ratio between guide book times and his or her own actual hiking times. Application of this personal "correction factor" usually makes it possible to accurately estimate probable time requirements for future hikes.

Beginning hikers, especially, sometimes overestimate their rate of travel and question the basic accuracy of guide book or signboard data as a result. It is important to realize that rough and winding trails with their frequent changes in grade are far more demanding of time and energy than road walking. Perception of elapsed time and distance can also be distorted by such factors as group size, numerous delays and diversions en route, high temperatures or humidity, and fatigue. It would be well, therefore, for beginners to rate their capabilities conservatively and to allow ample time for even the easiest hikes.

**Changes in the trail descriptions
will be published regularly in
The Long Trail News.**

**The News is the Club's quarterly newsletter
and is sent to all members.**

KEEP YOUR GUIDE BOOK UP TO DATE

EMERGENCIES

**In case of an emergency on the trail,
contact the Vermont State Police.**

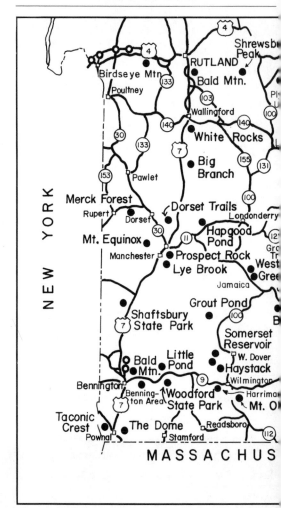

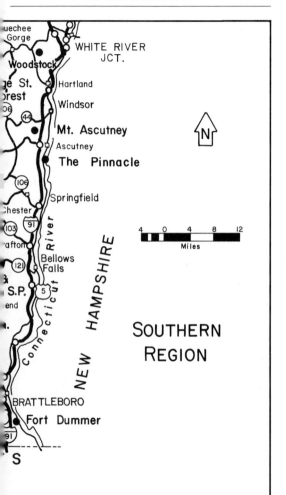

SOUTHERN REGION

Four of Vermont's six physiographic regions are represented in southern Vermont, which includes all of Bennington and Windham Counties, as well as parts of Rutland and Windsor Counties.

The Taconic Mountains lie along the western boundary of the state for about 75 miles between Massachusetts and the Lake Bomoseen area. Mt. Equinox is the highest peak in the range, which consists of mature, rounded mountains. The range is bordered on the east by the Valley of Vermont.

Forming a lowland between the Taconics and Green Mountains, the Valley of Vermont runs north from Massachusetts for about 85 miles to the vicinity of Brandon. Several miles wide in the Bennington area, the valley narrows to a few hundred yards in the vicinity of Emerald Lake. Otter Creek, the longest river entirely within Vermont, and the Batten Kill, a world famous trout stream, flow through the valley.

The Green Mountains occupy the central part of southern Vermont. A part of the Appalachian Mountain chain that extends from the southeastern U.S. to Canada, the range runs the length of the Vermont. Unlike the more northern part of the state, where they form two or more distinct parallel ranges, in southern Vermont the Green Mountains spread out in an irregular manner. Much of the area has long been relatively inaccessible and unsuitable for permanent settlement. As a result, more wild country is found in southern Vermont than anywhere else in the state except the Northeast Kingdom.

Between the Green Mountains and the Connecticut River is the Vermont Piedmont, which is the foothill region of the higher range. The Piedmont consists primarily of low hills, the result of extensive erosion. Mt. Ascutney, the highest peak in this region, rises some 2500 feet above the surrounding area.

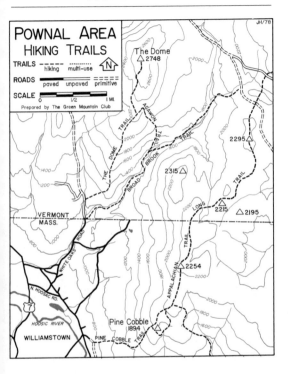

Broad Brook Trail

Maintained by the Williams Outing Club, this blue-blazed trail follows **Broad Brook** upstream from the Mass.-Vt. line to the **Long Trail**, south of the County Road (see USGS Williamstown, Pownal). During periods of high water it may be necessary to detour around some of the numerous stream crossings.

The trail approach is from Williamstown, Mass. From US 7, 0.8 m. south of the state line or 1.6 m. north of Mass. 2, follow Sand Springs Rd. and then Bridges Rd. east 0.6

m. to White Oaks Rd., which is followed 1.1 m. north to
the end of pavement at the state line. The trail begins a few
yards beyond at a gravel road to the right. Parking is
available near the trailhead.

From White Oaks Rd. (0.0 m.), the trail follows the water-
works road to the right, passes through a gate, and crosses
a sluiceway before entering the woods (0.2 m.) and following the brook on easy grades. Eventually crossing the brook
on the rocks (1.1 m.), the trail then follows the north bank
to a junction **(1.4 m.)**, where the **Agawon Trail** departs to
the left and ascends steeply to **The Dome Trail**.

Just above the junction, the **Broad Brook Trail** recrosses
the stream and continues along the south bank for some
distance before joining an old road from the right and again
crossing the brook (1.9 m.). Continuing past the foundations of an old mill (2.0 m.), the trail eventually ascends
steeply to the left away from the brook and the road (2.3
m.), crosses a side brook (2.4 m.), and then descends to
an old woods road near the main brook (2.5 m.). The trail
follows the road upstream for some distance and then makes
a final crossing of **Broad Brook** just below a small tributary
(2.9 m.).

Quickly crossing the side brook and climbing steadily,
the trail makes a second crossing (3.3 m.) and then continues its ascent to an old town road (3.6 m.). Bearing to
the right, the trail follows the old road on easy grades to
its terminus at the **Long Trail**, 2.6 m. north of the state line
(3.9 m.).

SUMMARY: White Oaks Rd. to Long Trail, 3.9 m.; 1220
ft. ascent; 2¾ hr. (Rev. 2 hr.).

The Dome

Although most of the broad ridge of this aptly named
mountain (see USGS Pownal) has a dense cover of spruce
and balsam, an exposed rock area on the summit offers good
views of the southern Green Mountains, the Hoosac Range
to the east, Mt. Greylock and the Berkshires to the south,
and the Taconic Range to the west. The red-blazed trail is
maintained by the Williams Outing Club.

The trail begins on the east side of White Oaks Rd., 0.3
m. north of the state line and the beginning of the Broad
Brook Trail, previously described. Limited parking is
available at the trailhead.

From White Oaks Rd. (0.0 m.), the trail follows a woods road, passes through two old fields, and then returns to the woods (0.2 m.). Following easy to moderately steep grades, the trail eventually reaches a junction on the right with the **Agawon Trail,** a few feet below **Meeting House Rock (1.2 m.).**

Beyond the junction, the trail climbs easily for some distance and then descends gradually to a shallow sag (1.7 m.), where it turns to the right and follows an occasionally muddy woods road. Leaving the road when it makes a sharp bend to the left (1.9 m.), the trail climbs steadily for some distance, passes through a wet area, and crosses a small stream (2.2 m.) before beginning a steep and circuitous climb over a series of quartzite outcrops to a false summit on a narrow ridge, from which there is a limited view through the trees (2.4 m.). The trail then makes a brief passage through a heavily wooded wet area before swinging to the east side of the ridge and climbing easily through scrub growth to the open **summit (2.6 m.),** at elevation 2748 ft.

SUMMARY: White Oaks Rd. to summit, 2.6 m.; 1650 ft. ascent; 2 hr. (Rev. 1¼ hr.).

Agawon Trail

With the Broad Brook Trail, this yellow-blazed trail maintained by the Williams Outing Club offers an interesting alternate return route from The Dome. From **The Dome Trail** at **Meeting House Rock,** 1.4 m. below the summit, the **Agawon Trail** ascends gradually toward the northeast on an old woods road. Soon turning sharply to the right (0.1 m.), the trail makes a steep and winding descent, crosses a small stream which later disappears underground (0.2 m.), and continues its steady winding descent to a wooded knoll overlooking Broad Brook (0.6 m.). Here the trail turns to the right and continues on easier grades to a junction with the **Broad Brook Trail,** a few yards below the latter's second brook crossing **(0.7 m.).** Via the Broad Brook Trail, it is 1.4 m. to White Oaks Rd., 0.3 m. south of The Dome trailhead.

SUMMARY: The Dome summit to White Oaks Rd. via Agawon Trail, 3.8 m.; 2 hr.

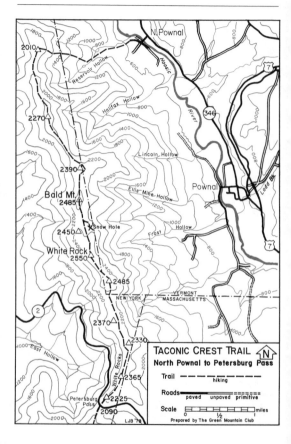

TACONIC CREST TRAIL
North Pownal to Petersburg Pass

Trail - - - -
        hiking

Roads
      paved   unpaved   primitive

Scale
        0   ½   1
                              miles

Prepared by The Green Mountain Club

Taconic Crest Trail

Maintained by the Taconic Hiking Club of Troy, New York, the trail follows the west and central ridges of the Taconic Range southward for about 30 miles from the Hoosic River at North Pownal to Berry Pond, in the Pittsfield (Mass.) State Forest. There are few trail signs, but the route is well marked with metal diamonds and white paint blazes. A trail guide with maps (1981) is available from the club (see Appendix).

The only Vermont portions of the trail are in the section between North Pownal and NY 2 at Petersburg Pass, just west of the NY-Mass. line (see USGS North Pownal, Berlin). Never far from the ridgeline, this section generally remains in mature hardwoods, but several large clearings and other vantage points offer wide views of the Adirondacks, Catskills, Taconics, and Berkshires. Water sources are scarce along the ridge, and camping is not permitted.

The northern terminus of the trail is the Hoosic River bridge, located on a street leading south from Vt. 346 at Powell's store in North Pownal village. Parking is available behind the store.

From the bridge (0.0 m.), the trail quickly turns to the right at an intersection and follows the paved road uphill to the west. Reaching the end of the public road just beyond several houses on the left (0.3 m.), the trail continues straight ahead along an old road through a large meadow, which provides views to the north. The trail soon enters pine woods (0.5 m.), passes through a small clearing (0.7 m.), and then bears left off the road opposite a small reservoir. A short distance beyond, the trail crosses **Reservoir Brook** and turns left onto a woods road **(0.8 m.)**.

The trail follows the road upstream into **Reservoir Hollow.** Soon after taking a sharp right onto another road (1.0 m.) and beginning a steady climb, the trail makes a second right turn (1.1 m.), climbs steeply past a green-blazed tree marking the **Vt.-NY boundary (1.5 m.)**, and then follows a series of short switchbacks through dense mountain laurel to a nameless summit (2010 ft.) at the north end of the ridge (1.8 m.).

Turning to the left, the trail follows easy up and down grades in a generally southerly direction along the broad and meandering ridge. After passing over two minor knobs (2.3 m. and 3.3 m.), the trail briefly returns to the Vt. side of the state line in the vicinity of a wooded knob (3.9 m.) and descends into the **saddle** north of **Bald Mt. (4.1 m.)**.

The trail then begins a steady climb to the wooded summit
(4.4 m.) and then continues around its east shoulder to a
spur which leads 250 feet to a lookout, where there are views
of the Pownal Valley, The Dome, and Mt. Greylock. The
main trail descends past two other lookouts to a sag (4.7
m.) and follows an old road uphill to a junction (4.9 m.).
To the left, a spur descends about 250 ft. to the east to **Snow
Hole,** a deep fissure in the rocks where tradition holds that
snow and ice may be found all year round.

From the Snow Hole spur, the trail continues uphill along
the old road, eventually crossing to the west side of the
ridge, bypassing the wooded summit of **White Rock,** and
passing through two large clearings (5.4 m. and 5.5 m.),
both offering good views to the west and south. Returning
to the woods after passing through two smaller clearings,
the trail continues with minor elevation changes to a
nameless peak (2485 ft.) on the Vt. side of the state line
(5.8 m.). The trail then descends across the boundary into
a wet sag (6.1 m.), climbs easily to the east of a wooded
peak (6.4 m.). Descending to a junction on the left with
the red-blazed **Birch Brook Trail (6.5 m.),** the trail continues
through an overgrown clearing (6.6 m.) before reaching the
north end of the extensive **White Rocks Clearing (6.8 m.).**
The open summit of **Jim Smith Hill (2330 ft.),** a few yards
east of the trail, offers extensive views to the south and west.

Soon returning to the woods (7.2 m.), the trail descends
steadily on a woods road to two small springs on the left
(7.4 m.). A short distance beyond, the trail turns to the right
off the road and rises to a large open area (7.7 m.). Descending in the open, the trail soon reaches NY 2 at the summit
of **Petersburg Pass,** opposite the Taconic Trails Ski Area
(7.8 m.). The trail continues through the ski area.

From Petersburg Pass, the highway descends about 4 m.
east to US 7, south of Williamstown, Mass. To the west,
it is about 5 m. to NY 22 at Petersburg.

SUMMARY: North Pownal to Petersburg Pass, 7.8 m.;
2520 ft. ascent; 5¼ hr. (Rev. 4½ hr.).

WATER IS PRECIOUS! Safeguard water supplies - the next hiker may be thirsty too.

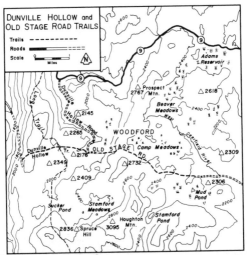

Dunville Hollow Trail

Maintained by the Pioneer Valley Section of the GMC, this blue-blazed trail offers some lengthy day trip possibilities in conjunction with the Long Trail and the Dunville Hollow Road (See USGS Bennington, Woodford).

From Vt. 9 (East Main St.) in Bennington, about 1 m. east of US 7, Burgess Rd. is followed uphill to the southeast for about 2.2 m. to a junction, where there is limited parking. Beyond this point, a jeep road takes the right fork and climbs steadily for 1.3 m. to a junction marking the beginning of the trail.

From the junction (0.0 m.), the **Dunville Hollow Trail** follows the left fork east and then north on the abandoned **Bennington-Heartwellville Road** to a junction (0.3 m.). Here the trail turns to the right and descends in an easterly direction to cross the **Long Trail (1.0 m.).**

To the north, the **Long Trail** continues for 2.0 m. to **Harmon Hill,** where there are good views of Mt. Anthony and Bennington to the west and limited views to the north of Bald Mt. and Glastenbury Mt. From Harmon Hill, it is 1.7 m. further to Vt. 9, about 5 m. east of Bennington and 0.2 m. west of the **Dunville Hollow Road.**

From the **Long Trail** crossing, the **Dunville Hollow Trail** descends to cross **Stamford Stream** on the rocks **(1.7 m.)** and then ascends to its terminus with the **Dunville Hollow Road** and the west end of the **Old Stage Road Trail (2.0 m.).** To the north, the **Dunville Hollow Road** descends along **Stamford Stream** past several camps for 3.0 m. to Vt. 9, from which point it is 0.2 m. west to the Long Trail and about 5.2 m. to Bennington.

SUMMARY: Burgess Rd. to Dunville Hollow Rd., 3.3 m.; 1030 ft. ascent; 2¼ hr. (Rev. 1¾ hr.).

Old Stage Road Trail

A continuation of the old **Bennington-Heartwellville Road,** this minimally maintained USFS trail begins at the junction of the **Dunville Hollow Trail** and the **Dunville Hollow Road,** 3.0 m. south of Vt. 9 (see USGS Woodford).

From the junction (0.0 m.), the trail ascends gradually to the east, crosses a wide logging road, and passes a camp on the left (0.3 m.) before climbing somewhat more steeply across a ridge (1.0 m.). Continuing for some distance with minor changes in elevation, the trail crosses a brook (1.8 m.) and then begins a gradual descent (2.2 m.), eventually reaching a camp on the left (3.3 m.). The trail then crosses **Reservoir Brook (3.4 m.),** crosses another brook (4.3 m.), and then crosses the West Branch of the Deerfield River just above a fork to the left (4.5 m.). A short distance beyond, the trail crosses **Yaw Pond Brook (4.7 m.).** The trail ends at a USFS road (4.9 m.) which leads 1.3 m. to the hamlet of Heartwellville (6.2 m.).

SUMMARY: Dunville Hollow Trail to Vt. 100, 6.2 m.; 570 ft. ascent; 3¼ hr. (Rev. 3½ hr.).

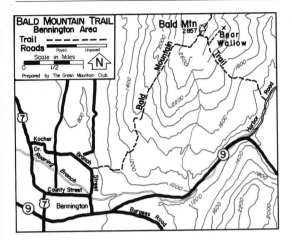

Bald Mt. Trail

This blue-blazed trail (see USGS Bennington) is one of the oldest continuously maintained trails in the area. Excellent views of the Bennington region may be seen from the ledges and old rock slides on the west slope, and wide views to the east, north, and south are provided from various points near the summit. The western branch of the trail between Bennington and the West Ridge Trail is rough and may be difficult to follow.

The trail begins on Branch St. in the northeast section of Bennington, where a power line crosses at a sharp turn. From Vt. 9 (East Main St.), about 0.8 m. east of US 7, Branch St. leads north to County St., where it bears sharply to the right, crosses Roaring Branch and continues to the unsigned trailhead (0.8 m.). From the north end of town, Kocher Dr. can be followed east from the traffic lights at the US 7-Northside Dr. interchange, past Park St. and Chapel Rd., for 1.2 m. Limited parking is available along the road at the trail junction.

From Branch St. (0.0 m.), the trail ascends a woods road parallel to the power line. After crossing two smaller lines, the trail crosses the wide clearing of a much larger **power line (0.3 m.)**, where there are views north and south. Following the road on easy grades and soon swinging to the north, the trail crosses a brook on a bridge (0.6 m.), and eventually bears to the left off the road (0.9 m.). After some distance, the trail crosses two small spring brooks (1.3 m.) and ascends through a "rock garden" between two diverging streams. The trail then crosses the stream at the point of diversion (1.7 m.) and continues to an open rock area deep in the woods beside the brook (1.9 m.).

Returning to the woods, the trail recrosses the brook (2.1 m.) and soon begins a steady climb to the right out of the hollow. After reaching a spur which leads 75 ft. left to a view of the Bennington area (2.7 m.), the trail continues its steady climb to cross the first of a series of old rock slides (2.9 m.), from which there are views of Bennington, Mt. Anthony, Lake Paran, Mt. Greylock, and the Taconics. Eventually returning to the woods (3.2 m.), the trail continues on easy grades and then turns to the left and climbs steadily, for the most part, toward the ridge. Soon after entering scrub growth, the trail continues in the open to a junction at ridgeline (4.0 m.).

To the left, the **West Ridge Trail** rises gradually to the summit of **Bald Mt. (4.1 m.)**. From the 2857 ft. summit there are views to the north of Glastenbury Mt., Mt. Equinox, and Dorset Peak.

From the junction (4.0 m.), the trail soon enters the woods and begins a descent via several switchbacks, soon passing a spur trail on the left (4.2 m.) which leads 0.2 m. to a spring at **Bear Wallow**. After continuing its winding descent for a distance, the trail finally takes a more direct route via an old road, crosses a small brook and soon reaches a better road bed. Bearing left and passing a camp (5.7 m.), the trail continues to a water tower in a grassy clearing and the dirt Woodford Hollow Road (5.9 m.). Limited parking is available in the field next to the tower. Take care not to block any of the nearby woods roads. To the right, the road leads south 0.8 m. to Vt. 9 at the Woodford Hollow Church, from which point it is 1.2 m. east to the Long Trail and about 4 m. west to Bennington.

SUMMARY: Branch St. to Bald Mt. summit, 4.1 m.; 2150 ft. ascent; 3 hr. (Rev. 2 hr.). Branch St. to public road, 6.1 m.; 2150 ft. ascent; 4 hr. (Rev. 3¾ hr.). Public road at water tank to summit only, 2.0 m.; 1580 ft. ascent; 2 hr. (Rev. 1¼ hr.).

Little Pond

This secluded pond (USGS Woodford) is reached by an unblazed and unsigned woods road which leaves the north side of Vt. 9 a short distance west of an old house on the height of land, 1.6 m. east of the Prospect Mountain Ski Area and about 1.6 m. west of Woodford State Park. A highway turnout is located a few hundred feet to the east, on the north side of the highway.

From the highway (0.0 m.), the road ascends through the woods to a power line crossing (0.5 m.), where there are views to the east and west. After dipping into a hollow, the road continues through overgrown fields past the remains of a camp (0.8 m.), where there is a wide view to the east of **Haystack Mt.** and the **Hoosac Range,** and then ascends gradually through the woods around a shoulder of **Hager Hill.** Reaching a fork on the left (2.4 m.), the road descends to the west shore of the pond (2.6 m.).

SUMMARY: Vt. 9 to pond, 2.6 m.; 330 ft. ascent; 1¾ hr. (Rev. 1¼ hr.).

Woodford State Park

Woodford State Park (campground, picnic area) is located on the south side of Vt. 9, about 11 m. east of Bennington and 3.2 m. west of Vt. 8. A blue-blazed trail around Adams Reservoir begins at the picnic area, located at the end of the first fork to the right beyond the park headquarters. A trail map is available at the park.

LEAVE NOTHING BUT FOOTPRINTS!

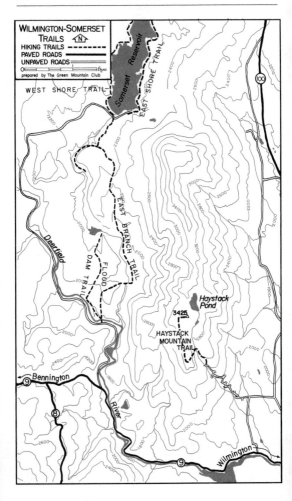

East Branch Trail

Maintained by the New England Power Company, this trail is marked with double yellow blazes except for a section on U.S. Forest Service land, which is marked with faded blue blazes. Since nearly all the trail is on power company property, hikers are reminded that overnight camping and open fires are prohibited. The trail begins on the gravel road to Somerset Reservoir, which leaves Vt. 9 about 1.5 m. east of its junction with Vt. 8 and 5.6 m. west of the traffic lights in Wilmington. Limited parking is available at the trail head, 2.1 m. north of Vt. 9.

Descending from the road (0.0 m.), the trail crosses the **West Branch** of the **Deerfield River** on a suspension bridge, and proceeds gradually uphill. The trail soon turns sharply uphill to the right at a junction with the **Flood Dam Trail (0.1 m.),** which departs to the left.

The East Branch Trail continues across a low ridge and crosses the **East Branch** of the **Deerfield River** on a suspension bridge (0.4 m.). The trail reaches an old railroad bed which it follows to the north. Along this roadbed are several scenic overlooks of the river as well as views of Mt. Snow to the northeast. The trail crosses several streams (1.2 m. to 1.6 m.), some of which can be easily crossed at fords or on hewn timbers which span the stream channel.

After crossing the last brook the trail bears to the right, leaves the railroad bed (1.6 m.), and crosses another brook on a hewn timber. The trail returns to the railroad bed (2.0 m.), crosses two more streams, and bears to the right off the main roadbed (2.3 m.). Following a spur railroad bed running up a stream, the trail quickly bears right, away from the river.

After crossing the brook (2.7 m.), the trail crosses a red-blazed boundary and enters the **Green Mountain National Forest (2.9 m.).** For the next 1.2 m. the trail is marked with blue blazes.

The trail follows the brook channel, crosses it (3.0 m.), bears right at the first fork in the brook (3.1 m.), and left at the second fork (3.2 m.). In this area, the trail is somewhat difficult to follow, so look carefully for blazes. The trail begins to level off and crosses the brook for the last time (3.3 m.). Descending across a red-blazed boundary line, the trail crosses back onto New England Power Company land (4.1 m.), where the double yellow blazes begin again. Here there are views of Mt. Snow and several beaver ponds.

The trail continues to descend gradually alongside a small stream into a large clearing (4.5 m.), where the **East Branch Spur Trail** leads left to the **East Branch** of the **Deerfield River.**

The main East Branch Trail turns sharply to the right at this junction and follows the upper edge of a small meadow. After returning to the woods (4.6 m.), the trail once again reaches the **East Branch (4.7 m.),** following its east bank for several hundred feet, then again turning away to the right. Climbing a moderate grade, the trail levels off and passes to the right of an old mill foundation (4.9 m.), then ascends to the right and reaches its terminus on the **Somerset Reservoir** access road (5.0 m.), just below the east end of the dam.

From the trail junction, the access road continues a few hundred feet uphill to the top of the dam, about 0.3 m. to parking and boat launching areas, and 0.5 m. to a picnic grove and the south end of the **East Shore Trail.** To the left of the East Branch Trail junction, the access road descends a short distance to the dam's outlet, 0.3 m. to the south end of the **West Shore Trail,** and 9.7 m. to Vt. 9.

SUMMARY: Road junction to Somerset Reservoir, 5.0 m.; 550 ft. ascent; 2¾ hr. (Rev. 2½ hr.).

Flood Dam Trail

Established and maintained by the New England Power Company, this trail diverges from the **East Branch Trail** 0.1 m. from the latter's southern terminus. It is marked with single yellow blazes.

A short distance from the **Deerfield River** suspension bridge, the Flood Dam Trail branches left where the **East Branch Trail** makes an abrupt right turn (0.0 m.). The Flood Dam Trail passes through overgrown clearings and woods along an old roadbed (0.1 m.), and continues parallel to the **Deerfield River** on level ground. The trail turns away from the river (0.4 m.) and continues to the base of a hill (0.5 m.), turning more northerly as it begins a gradual climb up a rocky section of trail. The trail climbs through mature hardwood forests to its highest point, located on the unmarked **Windham/Bennington County Line (1.2 m.).**

The trail continues generally northeasterly across this flat topped mountain, begins a very gradual descent and then levels out (1.7 m.). Turning sharply to the right, the trail descends again to the bottom of a hill, crosses a small stream

(1.8 m.), and continues northeasterly around a spruce and hardwood forest to another stream (1.9 m.). The trail meets an old railroad bed (2.0 m.) and turns sharply to the right, where there are views of a large area of beaver activity. The trail follows the railroad bed to its terminus at a picnic table on the shore of the pond (2.2 m.). The foundations of the old flood dam which dates back to at least the turn of the century can be seen from this point. The dam and railroad beds found in this area were associated with the valley's nineteenth century logging activity.

SUMMARY: Road junction to old flood dam and pond, 2.3 m.; ascent 280 ft.; 1¼ hr. (Rev. 1¼ hr.).

West Shore Trail

Established by the New England Power Company, this trail follows high ground on the west side of **Somerset Reservoir** to an indefinite terminus on the reservoir's shoreline. Especially near the north end, segments of the treadway are not yet clearly defined, and hikers should remain alert for indications of recent clearing and trail construction.

The trail begins at the junction of the access road and a chained service road at the base of the west end of the dam. Parking is available at the trailhead and other nearby locations. The route is marked with double yellow blazes.

From the access road (0.0 m.), the trail follows the service road up the face of the dam for about 400 ft. before turning left onto a woods road. Soon after leaving the road on the right (0.2 m.), the trail descends toward the reservoir, reaching the water's edge at a rock ledge (0.4 m.). The trail continues around two small coves (0.7 and 0.8 m.) and crosses a large brook entering another cove (1.3 m.) before rising to higher ground.

After returning to the shore and crossing another stream (1.7 m.), the trail again leaves the reservoir at a rocky cove (1.9 m.) and slabs the slope for some distance on occasionally rough ground before continuing with minor elevation changes to a former town road (2.5 m.). The trail follows the old road and its paralleling stone walls uphill to the left through an overgrown farm site (2.8 m.) and then descends gradually, bearing to the right at an old woods road junction (3.2 m.), and soon reaching a trail junction (3.3 m.). To the left, a red-blazed snowmobile trail follows old roads.

The West Shore Trail descends straight ahead on the right fork and soon returns to the reservoir (3.4 m.). Continuing along or near the shore, the trail crosses a large brook at the entrance to a cove (4.2 m.) and swings to the right away from a woods road which also uses the brook crossing. Once again turning into the woods (4.4 m.), the trail follows occasionally obscure routing a short distance inland, crosses a low spur ridge (4.9 m.), and gradually descends to the shore (5.2 m.). The trail follows the rocky beach for a short distance, returns to the shoreline, and then continues on higher ground to an ill-defined ending in the woods (5.6 m.).

SUMMARY: Access road to trail terminus, 5.6 m.; 3 hr. (Rev. 2¾ hr.).

East Shore Trail

Established and maintained by the New England Power Company, this trail follows high ground near the east shore of **Somerset Reservoir** and offers frequently changing views across the water of **Mt. Snow, Stratton Mt.**, and other area landmarks. The double yellow-blazed route utilizes, in part, a former woods road. The cleared trail ends on the shore opposite **Streeter Island,** and no attempt should be made to continue beyond this point.

The East Shore Trail begins in a picnic grove located at the end of the reservoir access road, about a half mile north of the dam. From the end of the road (0.0 m.), the trail crosses a small stream in the picnic grove and follows an old road to a cove. After swinging around the east end of the cove (0.2 m.), the trail leaves the reservoir and enters the woods, passes through a rock garden (0.8 m.), and crosses a small stream before returning to the reservoir at a small cove (1.0 m.), which is skirted on puncheon. Continuing across a tiny point to another cove (1.2 m.), the trail then returns to higher ground, crosses two low knolls (1.8 and 2.0 m.), and then descends to skirt another cove (2.1 m.).

Turning northerly on an old woods road, the trail turns left across a brook (2.3 m.) and slabs a slope. From the high point on the slope and an excellent view of the **Mt. Snow-Haystack Mt.** ridge, the trail descends to a clearing beside the shoreline (2.6 m.). Continuing in open woods near the shore, the trail crosses a large brook (3.4 m.) and enters another clearing at the shoreline (3.5 m.). The trail then descends gradually along the shore to its ill-defined ending in a shallow sag opposite **Streeter Island (4.2 m.)**.

SUMMARY: Access road to trail terminus, 4.2 m.; 2¼ hr. (Rev. 2¼ hr.).

Haystack Mountain

From the partially wooded conical summit (elevation 3425 ft.) there are local views of Haystack Pond and Mt. Pisgah (Mt. Snow) to the north; and Harriman Reservoir and Lake Sadawga to the south (see USGS Wilmington). More distant views include Mt. Ascutney to the northeast, Mt. Monadnock to the southeast, Mt. Greylock to the south, and Glastenbury Mt. to the north. For most of its length, this is a combination hiking, snowmobile, cross-country ski trail, and is marked with blue and orange plastic tags.

From Vt. 9, about 1.1 m. west of the traffic light in Wilmington and 5.8 m. east of Vt. 8, turn north onto Haystack Rd. (0.0 m.), continue past a road to the left (0.3 m.), and then turn left onto Chimney Hill Rd. at a staggered four-way junction (1.3 m.). At the next junction (1.6 m.), turn right onto Binney Brook Rd. and begin a steep and winding climb past several intersecting roads of the Chimney Hills development to the trailhead (2.7 m.), which is marked with a U.S.F.S. sign. Limited roadside parking is available in the vicinity.

From Binney Brook Rd. (0.0 m.), the trail trends to the northwest on an old road. The trail turns left from the woods road (0.4 m.) and ascends the ridge west of **Haystack Mt.** A blue-blazed spur on the right (2.0 m.) leads 0.4 m. to the summit. The snowmobile trail continues ahead to Haystack Ski Area.

SUMMARY: Road junction to summit, 2.4 m.; 980 ft. ascent; 1¾ hr. (Rev. 1¼ hr.).

Carry it out! Bring some plastic litter bags and carry out unburnable trash. Some areas are heavily used. Help keep them attractive for others to enjoy.

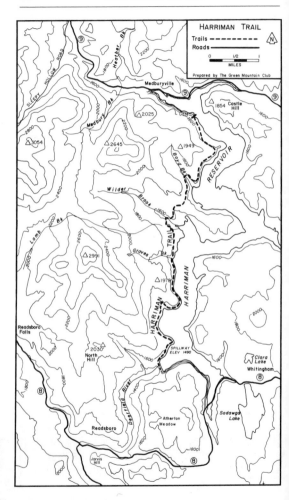

HARRIMAN TRAIL

Trails - - - - - - -
Roads

0   1/2   1
MILES

Prepared by The Green Mountain Club

Harriman Trail

Maintained by the New England Power Company, this trail follows unblazed but obvious routing along the west side of **Harriman Reservoir** between a small parking area at the base of **Harriman Dam** and a power company picnic area near the north end of the reservoir, west of Wilmington. In addition to providing frequent views across the reservoir of the surrounding mountains, the trail includes stone walls, foundations, and other reminders of past settlement along its route. Like all other recreational facilities on New England Power Company lands, this lengthy trail is open during daylight hours only. Overnight parking, camping, and open fires are not permitted.

Except for short bypasses of the original stream crossings, the trail follows the roadbed of the former Hoosac Tunnel and Wilmington Railroad. This section of track, with its roller coaster grades and a switchback crossing of Harriman Dam, was constructed in 1923 to replace original routing inundated by the newly created reservoir, and it remained in service until abandonment of the Readsboro-Wilmington portion of the line in 1937. The story of the railroad and related developments in the upper Deerfield valley is told in Bernard R. Carman's *Hoot, Toot and Whistle* (Stephen Green Press, 1963).

The northern terminus of the trail is the power company's Mountain Mills West picnic area. From Vt. 9, about 0.3 m. east of the Searsburg-Wilmington town line and 2.9 m. west of the traffic lights in Wilmington, cross the Deerfield River on a steel bridge. Turn left at a junction just beyond the bridge, and follow a narrow gravel road for one mile to the picnic area, where there is an impressive view of **Haystack Mtn.** The trail begins at a gate across the road.

The southern terminus is located at the **Harriman Dam.** From Vt. 100, about a mile west of the Whitingham post office and about 4 miles east of the center of Readsboro, turn north onto the paved Harriman Road and continue 1.9 m. to its end at a parking area at the bottom of a hairpin turn. The trail begins at an inconspicuous opening in the chain link fence. This access is located about 60 ft. to the left of the main gate, opposite a birch tree. The trail follows a paved road which crosses the lower face of the dam and then ascends to its top. Here the trail bears to the left onto the railroad bed and continues along the shore toward a prominent rock cut.

SOUTHBOUND DESCRIPTION: From the gate at the picnic area (0.0 m.), the trail and a coinciding truck road ascend steadily to the south. After passing camps on the right and left (0.8 m.), the trail continues the minor elevation changes, crosses a wire cable (1.1 m.), begins a brief swing to the west (1.6 m.), and then resumes a southerly course before crossing high above **Boyd Brook (1.9 m.).** The trail then passes through two prominent rock cuts and several less obvious ones before entering a much longer and deeper cut, where railroad ties are still in place (2.7 m.). Beyond the cut the trail reaches a junction (2.8 m.), at which point the truck road forks to the right and the trail bears to the left onto the undisturbed railroad bed.

Continuing through another cut (2.9 m.), the trail soon leaves the roadbed (3.0 m.) and descends to the right in the woods. Crossing **Wilder Brook** on a footbridge **(3.1 m.),** the trail follows an old woods road uphill to the left before turning to the right across a stone wall (3.2 m.) and continuing through an old farm clearing into a reforested area. Returning to the railroad bed (3.4 m.), the trail crosses the former stage road to Heartwellville (3.5 m.) and gradually approaches the reservoir. The trail then leaves the roadbed again (4.0 m.), descending to the left to cross **Graves Brook** a few feet from the reservoir (4.1 m.) and briefly following the shore before returning to the roadbed (4.3 m.).

After rounding a pleasant point (5.2 m.) and paralleling a long stone wall on the left, the trail swings to the right off the railroad bed (5.3 m.), briefly ascends in open woods, and then passes through an overgrown clearing near the massive foundations of former farm buildings. The trail then crosses a stone wall and turns to the left onto an abandoned town road (5.4 m.). Just before reaching the railroad bed once again, the trail turns to the right across a small nameless brook (5.5 m.). From the opposite bank, a short distance upstream, the trail swings to the left and descends into a grass-grown borrow pit. Here the trail resumes its route on the railroad bed.

**Protect Vermont's Hiking Trails
JOIN THE GMC**

Eventually passing through a prominent rock cut (6.4 m.), the trail descends gradually along the shore of the reservoir to the north end of **Harriman Dam (6.9 m.).** Here the trail jogs to the right for a few feet and then descends on a paved roadway which soon swings to the left and crosses the lower face of the dam to a closed gate in a chain link fence. The trail follows the fence to right for about 60 ft. to a white birch tree, at which point an inconspicuous narrow opening provides access to the parking lot (7.2 m.).

SUMMARY: Mountain Mills West picnic area to Harriman Dam parking area: 7.2 m.; 200 ft. ascent; 3¾ hr. either direction.

Mount Olga

From the old fire tower on the summit (USGS Wilmington), there are good views of southern Vermont, southwestern New Hampshire, and northern Massachusetts. The two trails to the summit, which make a loop, begin in Molly Stark State Park (picnic area, camping), located on the south side of Vt. 9, about 3½ m. east of Wilmington. Day visitors should make parking arrangements at the park headquarters.

Leaving the park road opposite the main building (0.0 m.), the blue-blazed main trail quickly crosses a small stream on a wooden bridge and climbs gradually to the east through the woods. After crossing stone walls (0.1 m. and 0.4 m.) the trail begins a steady climb through evergreens. Soon after being joined on the right by another blue-blazed trail (0.7 m.), the trail reaches the summit (elev. 2415 ft.) of **Mt. Olga (0.8 m.).** Two unmarked trails lead several hundred feet east to ski trails of the Hogback Mt. Ski Area, from which there are good views to the northeast.

From the previously mentioned junction just below the summit (0.0 m.), the blue-blazed **Mt. Olga Trail** descends through the woods, eventually reaching a junction with the **Stone Wall Trail (0.7 m.).**

The Stone Wall Trail leads to the right for 0.1 m., crosses a stone wall, then turns left and follows an old road bed between two stone walls for another 0.1 m. Passing a white-blazed trail on the left, the trail bears right to follow an unblazed path through an overgrown field to a small parking area (0.3 m.).

Continuing straight ahead at the junction, the **Mt. Olga Trail** follows blue blazes along the stone wall. At the end of the stone wall, the trail bears right and soon reaches the loop road in the camping area (0.9 m.). Bearing right, it is 0.2 m. to the park headquarters.

SUMMARY: Complete loop, 1.9 m.; 520 ft. ascent; 1¼ hr. (Rev. 1¼ hr.).

Fort Dummer State Park

A self-guiding nature trail, the blue and yellow-blazed **Sunrise Trail** begins a few feet north of the intersection of the main roads in the camping area, about a quarter mile above the park office. A main loop, nearly a mile in length, is supplemented by two short loop extensions, each about a quarter mile long. Two lookouts, one of which is reached by a short spur, overlook the Connecticut River and also offer views of Mt. Monadnock and the high terrain of the nearby New Hampshire-Massachusetts border country. A trail map is available at the park office.

Fort Dummer State Park is located a short distance south of Brattleboro. From a traffic light on U.S. 5, a quarter mile north of I-91 Exit 1 and 1.2 m. south of Vt. 9 West, follow Fairgrounds Road east past the high school. At an intersection near the bottom of a winding hill, turn right (0.5 m.) and follow South Main Street and its continuation, Old Guilford Road, to a dead end at the park (1.6 m.).

Shaftsbury State Park

Located 0.5 m. east of Vt. 7A in Shaftsbury and about 10.5 m. north of Bennington, Shaftsbury State Park has a combination nature and hiking trail that is about 1.5 m. in length.

The trail begins near the large group picnic shelter, circles the lake, and ends at the lake outlet near the contact station. A free pamphlet describing the trail is available at the park.

Your membership in the GMC supports hiker educational programs

Grout Pond Recreation Area

A major logging site until it was purchased by the Boy Scouts in 1950, Grout Pond was acquired by the U.S. Forest Service in 1979. The area is now managed as a multiple-use area providing dispersed recreation use including hiking and camping.

To reach the area from the east, follow the Arlington-West Wardsboro (Kelley Stand) Road west from Vt. 100 in West Wardsboro for 6.3 m. Turn left (south) on the Grout Pond access road and follow it 1.3 m. to the pond. From the west, follow the Arlington-West Wardsboro Road east from U.S. 7 in Arlington for about 12 m. to the access road.

The Forest Service maintains a number of blazed and signed hiking/cross-country ski trails in the area. There are several opportunities for loop hikes around the 70 acre pond, and two trails lead to Somerset Reservoir. Several cabins, shelters, and primitive tent sites are available for overnight use.

A USFS caretaker may be in residence during the summer and fall. Additional information and a trail map are available from the U.S. Forest Service, P.O. Box 1940, R.R. 1, Manchester Center, VT 05255.

TRAIL EROSION CONTROL

Erosion control on hiking trails takes many forms. Waterbars, made of log or stone, are placed across the trail at an angle to direct running water off the trail. Steps, also made of log or stone, are used to stabilize the trail on steep slopes and to keep soil from being carried downslope. Cribbing is used to hold the treadway in place where the trail crosses a steep side slope. Hikers can assist in erosion control by staying on the trail instead of walking around these structures.

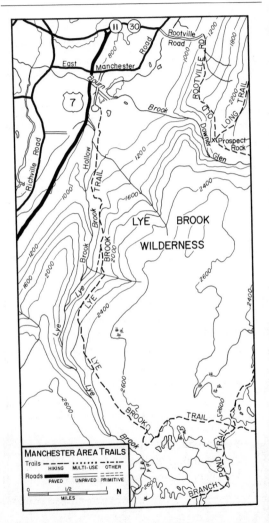

Lye Brook Trail

This blue-blazed USFS trail (USGS Manchester, Sunderland) passes through the heart of the Lye Brook Wilderness. Hikers are not required to obtain a permit for entry into this area. Because this trail passes through the Wilderness, it is more primitive than many other USFS trails.

From Vt. 11-30, 0.5 m. east of US 7 in Manchester Ctr., follow Richville Rd. south, turn left onto East Manchester Rd., and then right onto Glen Rd. Just past the first bridge, Glen Road goes to the left. Continue straight ahead for about ½ m. to a parking area.

From the parking lot (0.0 m.), the trail follows an old woods road through a clearing bearing to the right at a fork and continuing. The trail then begins a steady climb up Lye Brook Hollow some distance up the slope from the rotting ties of an abandoned logging railroad. After crossing a small stream (1.1 m.), the trail crosses the middle leg of a railroad switchback (1.5 m.) and then parallels the old railroad grade to another crossing (1.8 m.). To the right via the old grade, it is a short distance to a small stream and one of the higher waterfalls in Vermont.

From the upper railroad crossing, the trail continues along the old road, crosses two streams (2.3 m. and 2.5 m.), ignores a woods road to the left (3.2 m.), and eventually enters the woods at the end of the road (3.9 m.). Following easy grades and eventually assuming an easterly direction, the trail crosses a brook (4.8 m.), crosses another brook beyond a series of beaver ponds (5.9 m.), and passes over a low ridge before reaching the **Branch Pond Trail (6.9 m.)**, which leads south for 3.9 m. to the Arlington-West Wardsboro Rd. From the junction, the Branch Pond Trail leads north a short distance to the south end of **Bourn Pond (7.0 m.)**. To the north via the Branch Pond Trail, it is 3.5 m. to Prospect Rock and the upper end of the old Rootville Road.

SUMMARY: Road junction to Bourn Pond, 7.0 m.; 1950 ft. ascent; 4¾ hr. (Rev. 3¾ hr.).

Never underestimate the variability of Vermont weather! Always be prepared for rain and cold.

Prospect Rock

From this aptly named vantage point high above Downer Glen, there is a fine view of Mt. Equinox, Dorset Mt., and the Manchester area. Although not an official trail, the old Rootville Road, leading to a long forgotten hamlet in the town of Winhall, has been a popular hiking route for many years.

A few yards east of the junction of the East Manchester Road and Vt. 30, 2.5 m. from Manchester Ctr., the Rootville Road is followed 0.5 m. to its end. Parking is limited, and care should be taken not to obstruct the private driveway or the unmaintained section of the road.

From the end of the public road (0.0 m.), the abandoned and badly washed Rootville Road ascends steadily, following a flume-like stream for some distance and crossing several small streams. Eventually following easier grades and passing attractive young birches, the trail continues to a junction with the white-blazed **Long Trail (1.5 m.)**. Prospect Rock is about 200 ft. to the east via the Long Trail.

SUMMARY: End of public road to Prospect Rock, 1.5 m.; 980 ft. ascent; 1½ hr. (Rev. 1 hr.).

SPRING HIKING DISCOURAGED

The Green Mountain Club discourages hiking during the spring mud season, usually from mid-April to the end of May. Snow lingering at the higher elevations creates very wet and muddy conditions. Hiker's boots do much more damage to wet and muddy trails than when the trails are dry and more stable.

RESPECT PRIVATE LAND

Many of the trails in this book are located on private land. Use of these trails is made possible by the generosity and cooperation of these landowners, and is a privilege rather than a right. To comply with State law, and simply to respect private property:

Do not camp or build fires without landowner permission.

Carry out all litter. There are no trailside dumps.

Do not block driveways or roads. Leave all gates the way you found them.

Thank you! Your cooperation will help assure the continued existence of hiking trails on private lands.

EMERGENCIES

In case of an emergency on the trail, contact the Vermont State Police.

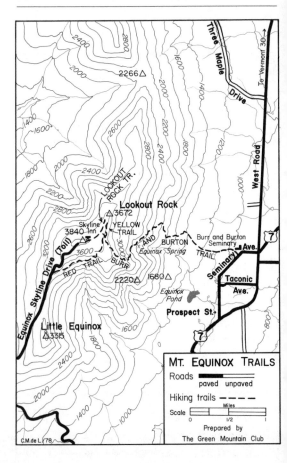

MT. EQUINOX TRAILS

Roads ▬▬▬▬ ——
paved unpaved

Hiking trails – – – –

Scale

Miles

0   1/2   1

Prepared by
The Green Mountain Club

C.M.de L./78

MOUNT EQUINOX

With an elevation of 3825 ft., Mt. Equinox (USGS Manchester) is the highest peak in the Taconic Mountains and also the highest peak in Vermont not in the Green Mountains. The origin of the mountain's name is still a source of debate, but common theory holds that it is a corruption of Indian words meaning either "place of fog" or "place where the very top is."

In addition to a hiking trail, access to the summit is provided by the paved Equinox Sky Line Drive (toll). From the parking area at the summit, local trails from the Sky Line Inn lead to several points of interest. The history of the mountain and the development of its facilities by the late Dr. Joseph C. Davidson is interestingly told in a free pamphlet available at the entrance to the Sky Line Drive, located on US 7 south of Manchester.

Burr and Burton Trail

Sporadically maintained by Burr and Burton students and marked with faded blue-blazes, the trail begins at the rear of Burr and Burton Seminary (a semi-private secondary school) in the village of Manchester. From the junction of US 7 and West Rd., just north of the green at the Mark Skinner library, follow Seminary Ave. west to Prospect St. Turn left on Prospect St. and continue a short distance to a driveway leading right into the school grounds. Ample parking is available opposite the entrance. To reach the trail, follow the driveway, ascend a path, and cross the south end of the athletic field to an old apple tree, where the first blaze can be seen.

From the athletic field (0.0 m.), the trail ascends through the woods on an old road, soon joins a road from the left (0.2 m.), and eventually bears to the left at a fork (0.4 m.). After a short climb, the trail crosses a woods road in a small clearing (0.6 m.).

From the crossing, the Burr and Burton Trail continues straight ahead and soon begins a steep and winding climb. Soon after reaching and following a much older woods road (1.2 m.), the trail passes between two large mossy rocks (1.4 m.) and continues to an unmarked spur **(1.6 m.)**, which descends about 200 ft. left to **Equinox Spring.** From the spur, the trail continues its steady climb to a shoulder of the mountain, where it makes a sharp swing to the right

(2.0 m.). Continuing on somewhat easier grades, the trail ascends through deep woods and eventually reaches a junction with the **Yellow Trail** and the **Red Trail (2.7 m.).**

To the right, the Yellow Trail, named for its blazing, follows easy grades northward for 0.5 m. to **Lookout Rock.**

To the left, a short distance beyond the Yellow Trail junction, the Red Trail descends steeply over the Devil's Wagon Road and then follows a rough up and down route past several views to the south to its terminus on Sky Line Drive, a short distance north of Little Equinox Mt. (1.0 m.).

Beyond the junction, the Burr and Burton Trail crosses an old road and continues through the woods a short distance to reach the ridge and a junction with the **Lookout Rock Trail (2.8 m.).** The summit, Sky Line Inn, and the summit parking lot, from which there are excellent views in most directions, are 0.1 m. to the left.

SUMMARY: Burr and Burton Seminary to summit, 2.9 m.; 2870 ft. ascent; 3 hr. (Rev. 1½ hr.).

Lookout Rock Trail

From the Sky Line Inn, this trail descends to the north along the ridge past the upper end of the Burr and Burton Trail (0.1 m.) and a granite memorial to Mr. Barbo, one of Dr. Davidson's faithful dogs, to **Lookout Rock (0.4 m.)** and a junction with the Yellow Trail. From Lookout Rock, there are excellent views to the north and east overlooking the Manchester area, Mts. Ascutney and Monadnock, and the White Mountains.

Sending in your reports of trail conditions will help the GMC keep this guide book up to date, and keep hikers advised of hiking conditions. Please fill out and mail the form in the back of this book.

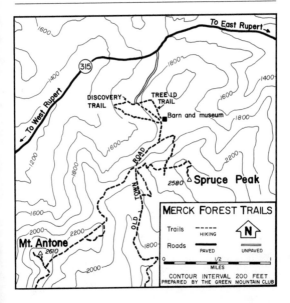

MERCK FOREST

Located in the town of Rupert, the Merck Forest (USGS Pawlet) consists of more than 2600 acres of abandoned farmland devoted to forestry, education, and recreation. The forest is open to public use during daylight hours throughout the year, but permission must be obtained in advance to camp at any of the several sites provided. There are no fees for use of the area, but donations, left in the contribution boxes at each entrance, are appreciated.

The trails described below are part of an intricate network of more than 26 miles of forest roads and trails providing access to all parts of the forest. Closed at all times to motorized vehicles, most are ideally suited for walking and cross-country skiing. A free map of the trail system is available at the parking area, which is reached by following a gravel road south from a Merck Forest sign at the height of land on Vt. 315, between Rupert and East Rupert.

Mount Antone

From the parking area (0.0 m.), the trail follows Old Town Road past sweeping views to the south to the Barn and the upper end of the Discovery Trail (0.3 m.). After descending for some distance, the road ascends through the woods to a junction with Hunting Lodge Road and the Mt. Antone Trail (0.8 m.).

From the junction, the Mt. Antone Trail takes the right fork and follows easy grades along the ridge, passes through **Clark Clearing (1.3 m.)**, and continues to a shelter at a junction (1.4 m.), where the Clark Clearing Road departs to the left and a ski trail (which offers alternate routing) leaves on the right. The Mt. Antone Trail continues straight ahead and soon begins a steady, winding climb to the left of the ridge. After regaining the ridge, the trail continues on easier grades, is rejoined on the right by the ski trail (1.9 m.), and then begins a steady ascent past the Wade Lot Road and Lookout Road (2.1 m.) to a junction with the Masters Mountain Road and the **Beebe Pond Trail (2.3 m.)**. Here the Mt. Antone Trail turns sharply to the right and ascends steeply to a junction with a spur trail, which leads left 0.1 m. to a lookout. A short distance beyond, the main trail reaches the 2620 foot summit (2.5 m.), where there are views of Dorset Peak, the southern Adirondacks and northern Catskills, and the White Creek valley.

SUMMARY: Parking area to summit, 2.5 m.; 820 ft. ascent; 1¾ hr. (Rev. 1¼ hr.).

Spruce Peak

The trail to Spruce Peak begins at the junction of Old Town Road and Hunting Lodge Road, 0.8 m. from the parking area. From the junction (0.0 m.), the trail enters the woods and soon begins a winding ascent to a junction (0.4 m.). To the right, a spur leads about 300 ft. to a clearing, where there is a good view of Mt. Antone. To the left, a trail descends 0.3 m. to Gallup Road, from which point it is 0.4 m. to the Barn.

From the junction, the trail slabs through the woods to Lodge Road, which it follows to the left for a short distance before turning sharply to the right (0.5 m.) and beginning a steep and winding climb to the summit (0.7 m.). From the open rock, there is a fine view of Mt. Antone and the Merck Forest area.

SUMMARY: Road to summit, 0.7 m.; 635 ft. ascent; ¾ hr. (Rev. ½ hr.).

Merck Nature Trails

Two self-guided nature trails, the Discovery Trail and Tree Identification Trail, begin at the upper parking lot and end near the Barn. Trail guides can be borrowed at the starting points.

Hapgood Pond Nature Trail

The USFS Hapgood Pond Recreation Area (picnic area, campground, swimming) is reached from the village of Peru, located a short distance to the north of Vt. 30, east of the Bromley Mountain Ski Area. In the village, bear left on the blacktop Hapgood Pond Road. Continue for 1.7 m. to the entrance of the Recreation Area. The **Land and Man Forest Trail**, 0.8 m. long, circles the pond.

The U.S. Forest Service and Vermont Department of Health remind us that any water supply can become contaminated. Therefore, the purity of water supplies cannot be guaranteed unless water is first filtered, boiled, or chemically treated.

GMC membership supports the maintenance of over 400 miles of hiking trails in Vermont

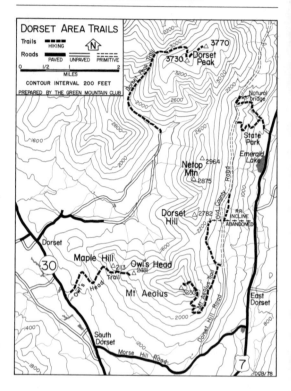

Dorset Peak

Although this mountain (USGS Dorset) is one of New England's one-hundred highest peaks, the summit (3770 ft.) is wooded and provides only limited views. The trail is not marked or maintained, and the last half mile is overgrown in places.

From the village of Dorset, just west of the Barrows House, follow a paved road north, turn right at the next junction

(0.7 m.), and continue past a fork to the left (0.9 m.). Continue beyond the end of pavement (1.7 m.) to the end of the public road in Dorset Hollow (4.2 m.). Special care should be taken not to block any of the driveways or roads in the area.

From a stream crossing at the end of the public road (0.0 m.), the trail ascends easily on an old woods road, staying within sight or sound of the brook to the left, and soon reaches the debris from the flood and landslides which ravaged the Dorset Hollow area in late 1976. Crossing the stream (0.8 m.), the trail crosses another brook from the left, just below a camp (1.1 m.). The trail stays to the right of the camp, briefly passes through uncleared flood debris, and then begins an increasingly steep climb along the road on the left side of the brook. Eventually skirting the base of two slides (1.6 m.), the trail continues its steady climb along the woods road, passes a large white boulder on the right (2.0 m.), and then continues on easier grades to a junction in the saddle (2.2 m.). To the left, a woods road descends to a public road south of Danby Four Corners.

From the saddle, the trail turns to the right and follows an old road northeasterly on easy grades. After crossing the second of two small streams at the ruins of an old shed (2.4 m.), the trail bears right (2.5 m.), and climbs steeply to an obscure junction (2.8 m.). The trail turns to the right and makes a steep ascent to a small clearing and the remains of a fire tower on the mountain's **middle peak (3730 ft.) (2.9 m.).** Continuing in a northeasterly direction, the trail crosses a shallow sag and reaches the wooded **summit (3.4 m.).**

SUMMARY: Public road to summit, 3.4 m., 2320 ft. ascent; 3 hr. (Rev. 1¾ hr.).

Owl's Head Trail

The present trail (USGS Manchester, Dorset) is a restored remnant of a lengthy loop created about 50 years ago to link Owl's Head, Mt. Aeolus, Dorset Peak, and other significant summits surrounding Dorset Hollow. Minimally maintained, the trail is poorly marked and ill defined in places. Several vantage points offer a variety of local and distant views.

The trail begins on a gravel spur loop on the north side of Vt. 30, 1.3 m. from the Dorset Inn in Dorset and 1.4 m. from South Dorset village. Roadside parking is available.

From the spur road (0.0 m.), the trail ascends a wide gravel road, bears to the right onto an older road (0.3 m.), and then makes another right turn at the next road junction (0.6 m.). The trail then continues on easy grades to a deer camp (1.0 m.), where it turns sharply to the left and soon encounters the first of the occasional orange flags. After crossing an old woods road (1.3 m.), the trail ascends steadily to the open face of an abandoned marble quarry (1.4 m.). The quarry dump on the left offers limited views to the southwest.

From the quarry, the trail bears right and within 150 ft. turns left, then ascends steeply for another 150 ft. to the first road on the right. The trail now ascends at a moderate grade along an old road with limited views to the south and reaches a flat-topped ridge (1.9 m.) which provides a good view of Owl's Head. Crossing the saddle between Maple Hill and Owl's Head (2.1 m.), the trail turns sharp left at a huge boulder on the right. A steep zigzag climb up the cliff ends at **Gilbert Lookout (2.2 m.),** named for the father of the Dorset area trails, George Holly Gilbert.

SUMMARY: Vt. 30 to Gilbert Lookout, 2.2 m.; 1260 ft. ascent; 1¾ hr. (Rev. 1 hr.)

Mount Aeolus Trail

Unmaintained but well defined, this trail provides a route to the summit of Mt. Aeolus from the east. For guide book purposes, the quarry roads leading to the trail are considered part of the trail.

From South Dorset, on Vt. 30, follow the paved Morse Hill Road 2.5 m. to the Dorset Hill Road on the left. From a state historical marker on US 7, about a mile south of East Dorset, the same Morse Hill Road leads 1.2 m. to this junction. From Morse Hill Road, follow the unpaved Dorset Hill Road 1.9 m. to an obscure road on the left, just beyond a white house. A sign at this junction states that the side road is open to the public. Roadside parking is available in the vicinity.

From the junction, the Dorset Hill Road continues northward and crosses an abandoned inclined railway grade (0.4 m.). The road now becomes the abandoned Old County Road, passes a trail on the right leading to Emerald Lake State Park (1.6 m.), reaches another Emerald Lake trail (2.4 m.), and continues beyond the

Natural Bridge (3.0 m.) for some distance before eventually again becoming a maintained road leading to Danby.

The Mount Aeolus Trail takes the left fork at the junction (0.0 m.) and soon reaches a fork (0.1 m.). Straight ahead, the road continues 1.0 m. to the Freedley quarry. The Mount Aeolus Trail turns sharply to the left and follows an old quarry road southerly. Bearing to the right at a fork (1.1 m.), a short distance beyond two quarry spurs to the right, the trail ascends to a clearing and the first quarry operated in the United States (1.3 m.). Good views of the Manchester area and Bromley Mt. are available from quarry dumps.

A short distance beyond the quarry, the trail turns to the right at a road junction and ascends steadily above the roofless quarry to another road junction (1.7 m.). Here the trail turns to the right and climbs past the entrance to **Mt. Aeolus Cave (2.0 m.),** which is easily overlooked. Because of the vital importance of this cave as a place of hibernation for the endangered Indiana Bat, an iron gate has been built at the cave entrance to minimize disturbance of these timid creatures by humans.

A short distance above the cave, the trail passes a lookout on the right and then turns to the left off the road (2.1 m.). Marked with plastic flagging, the trail mostly follows old logging roads to the summit of **Mt. Aeolus (2.7 m.).** A spur to the left leads about 50 ft. to a lookout with views of the Dorset-Manchester area, Stratton Mt., Haystack Mt., Mt. Equinox, and Mt. Greylock.

SUMMARY: Dorset Hill Road to summit, 2.7 m.; 1850 ft. ascent; 2½ hr. (Rev. 1¾ hr.).

Emerald Lake State Park

Emerald Lake State Park (picnic area, campground, swimming) is located on US 7 in North Dorset. In addition to the trails mentioned below, several shorter trails are shown on a trail map of the park, available without charge.

A **Nature Trail,** somewhat more than a half mile long, begins near the contact station and ends near the beach area. A free nature trail guide is available at the park.

From the access road, a short distance north of the contact station, the blue-blazed **Ledge Trail** heads easterly to cross the railroad tracks under the highway bridge, then turns to the south and climbs through the woods to ledges

above the highway (0.6 m.). Here there is a good view of
Emerald Lake and Netop Mt. An unofficial extension
(unblazed) continues 0.4 m. south to a gravel pit and US 7.

Natural Bridge Trail

Unblazed but easy to follow, the trail unofficially begins
just west of US 7 at the entrance to Emerald Lake State Park.
The road can be driven a short distance to a private house
and the official beginning of the trail, but it is suggested
that cars be left below or in the state park.

From the state park entrance (0.0 m.), the trail follows
the public road west to its ending at a private house (0.1
m.). Climbing easily at first, the trail continues on an abandoned town road, passing two old dams in the brook to
the left before reaching a fork (0.3 m.), where a trail to the
left ascends through the state park to the old County Road.
The Natural Bridge Trail takes the right fork and soon begins
a steep and winding climb. Eventually swinging sharply
to the left at a fork (0.6 m.), the trail continues on somewhat
easier grades, crosses two brooks (1.0 m. and 1.1 m.), and
then resumes its steady climb. The trail takes the left fork
at the next junction (1.2 m.) and continues on easier grades
to the old **County Road (1.4 m.).**

Turning to the right, the trail follows the old County Road
to a junction on the right, about 150 ft. before a brook crossing (1.6 m.). Here the trail descends downhill for 150 ft.
to the **Natural Bridge,** which spans the narrow gorge of
the brook.

SUMMARY: State park entrance to Natural Bridge (1.6
m.); 900 ft. ascent; 1¼ hr. (Rev. ¾ hr.).

Grafton Area Trails

The numerous scenic and historical attractions of the
Grafton area (USGS Saxtons River) are described in a
brochure and map, available for twenty cents from the
Grafton Historical Society. The guide describes nine walks,
which are up to ten miles long and follow the local town
roads.

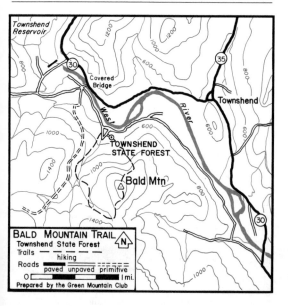

Bald Mountain

Located in Townshend State Forest (campground), the summit, once occupied by a fire tower, has several small clearings offering views of the Townshend reservoir and West River Valley, Stratton Mt., Bromley Mt. and Mt. Monadnock in southwestern New Hampshire (see USGS Saxtons River).

The blue-blazed loop trail begins and ends in the Townshend State Park campground. The park is reached by taking Vt. 30 north from Townshend village for about 2.0 m. to Townshend Dam. From the north, follow Vt. 30 south from the white steepled church in West Townshend until the dam is in sight. At the dam turn west and cross the spillway on a narrow bridge and continue straight to an intersection. Turn left onto the dirt road, which leads past the Scott covered bridge (the longest single span covered bridge in Vermont). Bear right at the bridge and continue parallel to the West River to the park entrance. There is a small day use fee charged at the park. Parking is available near the main building.

From the parking area (0.0 m.), the trail follows the campground loop road left. At the end of the campground loop near campsite #6, the trail leaves the road next to a large white pine tree and ascends eastward, soon beginning a steep climb. The trail bears right (0.5 m.) and ascends at a more moderate grade through a stand of hemlocks. After crossing an intermittent brook (0.8 m.), the trail follows a gentle grade below the ridge with occasional views of the West River Valley, Townshend Dam and distant mountains. Beginning a steeper ascent, the trail turns sharply left (1.2 m.) and ascends to the summit of **Bald Mt. (1.4 m.)**.

From the summit, the trail descends gradually to the south and soon approaches an alder swamp on the left (1.7 m.). Swinging to the southwest the trail continues to descend to a right turn (1.9 m.). The trail passes several small cascades along the brook, crosses and recrosses the brook, and passes an old cellar hole (2.0 m.). After joining the remnants of an old logging road the trail passes through a hemlock forest, makes several switchbacks, crosses a recently used logging road and bears to the right (2.5 m.).

Continuing its descent, the trail soon reaches **Negro Brook.** After crossing the brook on rocks (2.8 m.), the trail follows an old woods road steadily downhill. Crossing the brook again, this time on a wooden bridge (3.0 m.), the trail soon reaches the paved park road. Turning right on this road completes the loop at the parking lot (3.1 m.).

SUMMARY: Complete loop, 3.1 m.; 1,100 ft. ascent; 2 hr. (Rev. 2 hr.).

Ledges Overlook Trail

Maintained by the U.S. Army Corps of Engineers, this recently established trail begins and ends at a wooded picnic grove located on the west shore of **Townshend Reservoir,** 0.6 m. from a public road which leaves Vt. 30 and the dam between Townshend and West Townshend. The trail is blazed with yellow Corps of Engineers logos on a green background. A short section of the paved access road separates the two ends of the trail; thus the two trail signs refer to the same trail.

From the access road (0.0 m.), the trail quickly crosses a parallel dirt road and begins a steady ascent to the north and northwest on an old woods road. After passing old foundations on the left, the trail bears left off the road (0.2 m.) and soon reaches and follows another road on easier grades. After resuming a steady climb, the trail turns sharply left off the woods road (0.6 m.) and ascends easily in a southerly direction well below the ridgeline. Reaching its highest point on a spur ridge (0.8 m.), the trail briefly descends on an old road and then turns left to zig-zag into an old clearing at the top of a **rock ledge (0.9 m.).** From this vantage point, there is a panorama of Townshend Reservoir, the dam, the Scott covered bridge, Bald Mt., and other features of the West River Valley.

From the lookout, the trail ascends to the right and soon rejoins the woods road. Descending steadily at times to the south, the trail soon turns sharply left, crosses a stone wall (1.1 m.), and descends to the northwest below a shoulder of the ridge. Diverging to the right off the road (1.2 m.), the trail continues through the woods for a short distance, then rejoins the road (1.4 m.), and continues beside old stone walls. Soon after crossing another wall and a road just to the left of a woods road junction, the trail reaches its lower terminus on the access road (1.5 m.), about 400 feet below its starting point.

The hiking times in this book are not necessarily those you will or should take. They are calculated with a formula (pg. 22) and are included only to serve as a guide.

West River Valley Greenway

Owned by the Conservation Society of Southern Vermont, the area consists of about 3000 acres along the West River in the towns of Jamaica and Londonderry. Several marked and unmarked trails are shown and described in a guide, available for fifty cents from CSSV, RR 1, Newfane, Vermont 05345. It is strongly recommended that a topographic map (USGS Londonderry) be used in conjunction with the guide.

Hamilton Falls

Beginning in **Jamaica State Park** (day use fee) and continuing into the **West River Valley Greenway**, this unmarked but obvious route (USGS Londonderry) follows the roadbed of the former **West River Railroad** for about two miles before ascending to one of the highest and most spectacular waterfalls in Vermont. A trail brochure, including a map, is available at the park.

Conceived as a connecting link between the Connecticut River and Lake Champlain, the West River Railroad operated from 1879 to 1935 between Brattleboro and South Londonderry, first as a narrow gauge line and later as a standard gauge railroad. Much of the route from Jamaica southward remains well defined, with many sections of roadbed and several bridge abutments being readily visible from Vt. 30. The story of the West River is told in Victor Morse's *36 Miles of Trouble*.

The trail begins at the state park swimming area, 0.3 m. from the contact station. From a gate at the end of the state park road (0.0 m.), the trail follows the old railroad grade upstream and passes a series of wire cables across the river (0.5 to 0.8 m.), which are used for setting slalom courses for kayak races. The trail continues past an unsigned junction on the right (0.9 m.) with the blue-blazed trail to **Adam Pond**, crosses several small streams, passes old foundations in thick undergrowth on the left (1.6 m.), and then skirts the posted boundary of private property for some distance before reaching an old road on the right (1.9 m.). Here a single blue blaze marks the beginning of the route to **Hamilton Falls**.

The old railroad bed continues straight ahead, crosses Cobb Brook on the rocks beside ruins of bridge abutments (2.0 m.), and then degenerates into a foot trail as it reaches the base of the **Ball Mountain Dam (2.2 m.)**. An unmarked minimally maintained, and often obscure CSSV trail continues from the seismograph station to the top of the dam and then slabs around the rocky south face of Shatterack Mountain for some distance before returning to the river valley; however, this should be regarded as a bushwhack route.

Leaving the **railroad bed (1.9 m.)**, the trail to **Hamilton Falls** turns to the right and ascends steadily on the old road, high above **Cobb Brook**, to an unmarked junction on the left (2.8 m.). Here a spur slabs downhill for about 325 ft. to the base of **Hamilton Falls**, beyond which point it is unsafe to venture. The main trail continues on the old road to a junction with a narrow public road (3.0 m.). Here the trail follows the road downhill to the left past a sawmill and soon turns to the left onto a footpath which leads about 250 ft. to the top of **Hamilton Falls (3.1 m.)**. As noted by the prominent signs, these spectacular falls should be enjoyed with great caution — at least ten people have died here in recent years.

SUMMARY: State Park swimming area to fall, 3.1 m.; 700 ft. ascent; 2 hr. (Rev. 1½ hr.).

Adam Pond

Adam Pond, better known locally as Bloodsucker Pond, is reached by a blue-blazed trail which leaves the **West River Railroad** bed at an unsigned junction located 0.9 m. upstream from the **Jamaica State Park** swimming area. Short trails connect the pond with a nearby ridge on the west, where there are outstanding views of Jamaica and the West River valley from the summit area.

From the railroad bed (0.0 m.), the trail climbs a bank on the right and ascends steadily southward on an old woods road. Turning left off the road into a shallow sag (0.2 m.), the trail continues on easier grades to the north end of **Adam Pond (0.3 m.)**, where it swings to the right and follows the shore to the base of a ledge (0.5 m.). The trail winds its way to the top of the ledge, descends to the pond (0.6 m.), and continues along the shore to the pond's inlet (0.7 m.). Leaving the pond, the trail continues to the **Jamaica State Park** camping area **(1.3 m.).**

SUMMARY: Railroad bed to Adam Pond inlet, 0.7 m.; 150 ft. ascent; ½ hr. (Rev. ½ hr.). Railroad bed to Jamaica State Park, 1.3 m.; 150 ft. ascent; ¾ hr. (Rev. ¾ hr.).

Big Branch Trail

This USFS trail descends to the Big Branch river from the Big Branch Picnic Area in the Green Mountain National Forest, White Rocks National Recreation Area.

To reach the trailhead follow USFS Road 10 east from the village of Danby for 3.0 m. to the picnic area, located on the south side of the road.

The picnic area offers a good vantage point high above **Big Branch** with a sweeping southwestern view of the Otter Creek Valley and Dorset Peak. The Big Branch Trail begins at a break in the rail fence near this vista, and descends steeply via switchbacks to the boulder filled river (0.1 m.).

When parking vehicles at trailheads and road junctions, hikers should take special care to avoid obstructing traffic or blocking access to homes, farms, or woodlots. Vandalism can be a problem at some trailhead parking areas, and it may be wiser to leave your car in town, especially if you will be out overnight.

**SUPPORT VERMONT'S TRAILS
JOIN THE GMC**

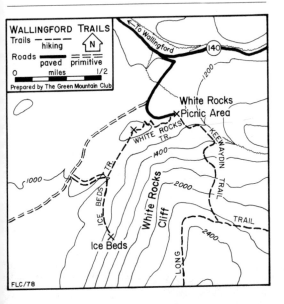

White Rocks Trail

This trail, as well as the Keewaydin and Ice Beds trails described later, begins in the USFS **White Rocks Picnic Area.** From US 7 in Wallingford, follow Vt. 140 east. Bear right at a fork (2.1 m.), and then take the next right turn (2.2 m.), and continue to the parking area (2.7 m.).

From the west side of the parking area (0.0 m.), the blue-blazed trail quickly crosses a small stream and soon reaches the base of a rocky hogback. From here, the trail follows a series of switchbacks to a saddle (0.2 m.). To the left, a spur leads a few feet to the Parapet, where there is an impressive view of the White Rocks Cliffs.

From the saddle, the trail ascends past another view of
the cliffs to the top of the knoll and the beginning of the
Ice Beds Trail (0.3 m.). Here there is a good view to the
west of the Otter Creek valley and the Taconics beyond.

SUMMARY: Picnic area to summit. 0.3 m.; 160 ft.
ascent; ½ hr. (Rev. ¼ hr.).

Ice Beds Trail

The blue-blazed Ice Beds Trail descends from the knoll
and reaches a woods road (0.2 m.). Turning left and following this road the trail descends to cross a brook (0.4 m.),
and then quickly reaches a second, smaller brook. After
crossing this brook the trail follows it upstream to its source
in the **Ice Beds** at the base of an old rock slide **(0.5 m.)**.
A nearby USFS interpretive sign explains the origin of the
term.

SUMMARY: White Rocks Cliff Trail to Ice Beds, 0.5 m.;
260 ft. descent; ¼ hr. (Rev. ½ hr.).

Keewaydin Trail

From the upper end of the White Rocks Picnic Area (0.0
m.), this blue-blazed trail ascends steadily to the south and
then swings to the left on easy grades. The trail resumes
its steady climb high above Bully Brook and its numerous
cascades. After crossing a small stream, the trail turns sharply to the right and begins a swing around a spruce and
hemlock covered promontory, then continues its steady
climb to a junction with the **Long Trail (0.8 m.)**.

To the left, the white-blazed Long Trail descends to the
north through the woods, passes **Greenwall Shelter (1.3
m.)**, and eventually reaches a clearing (1.9 m.). The Trail
then passes a house and continues on a gravel road to **USFS
Road No. 19 (2.2 m.)**. To the left, it is about 1.5 m. to Vt.
140 and about 2.0 m. back to the White Rocks Picnic Area.

SUMMARY: Picnic area to Long Trail, 0.8 m.; 1200 ft.
ascent; 1 hr. (Rev. ½ hr.).

BIRDSEYE MOUNTAIN

The Birdseye Hiking Trails were established in 1979 as a service project by Camps Betsey Cox, Killoleet, Keewaydin and Sangamon. Their names have been applied to four of the dozen lookouts and points of interest located on or near the four summits on the Birdseye Mountain Park property. Castle Peak, the highest of these summits, is slightly over 2000 ft. in elevation.

The Park is located on the south side of route 4A, 2.6 m. west of West Rutland. The trails on the summit ridge are interconnected to provide opportunities for trips of varying length. Except for short sections of the North Peak and Castle Peak Trails, grades are not overly steep, and the footway generally is firm and dry.

North Peak Trail

In addition to providing access to three impressive lookouts on the northernmost summit of the ridge, this trail serves as the approach to the Butterfly and Castle Peak Trails. From the Base Lodge (0.0 m.) the trail trends westerly on an old service road. At a sharp left turn in the road (0.1 m.) the trail continues straight ahead, ascending through an old clearing and then entering pine woods. Immediately after crossing a telephone line and a power line clearing (0.2 m.), the trail enters mixed hardwoods and assumes a southerly direction.

After crossing a normally dry brook bed (0.3 m.), the trail ascends on easy grades and eventually reaches a well-defined woods road (0.5 m.), which it follows around a shoulder of the mountain. Soon after the road turns to the left and levels out, the trail bears right (0.7 m.) and rises through open woods to cross a woods road (0.9 m.). Climbing easily, the trail soon crosses another woods road (1.0 m.), at which point it enters and follows another road which ascends steadily at moderately steep grades. Meeting and crossing yet another well-used road, the trail begins a short but steep climb to a switchback at **Killoleet Rock (1.3 m.)**, where there is a tunnel view to the west. Here the trail turns sharply to the left and begins a slabbing climb to the north, crosses an overgrown road (1.4 m.), and continues on easier grades to **Keewaydin Ledge (1.5 m.)**, where there is a more extensive view to the west. Here the trail bears to the right and ascends gradually into a sag to **North Peak Junction**

(1.6 m.), at which point the Butterly and Castle Peak Trails leave on the right.

Continuing straight ahead, the North Peak Trail quickly reaches the beginning of a loop which circles the summit of North Peak. Bearing to the right the trail continues a short distance to a spur which leads right about 50 feet to **East Birdseye Lookout,** overlooking the pastoral Castleton River valley and the communities of West Rutland, Proctor, and Rutland. From the Lookout, the main trail quickly passes over the highest point on North Peak to a spur which leads a few feet to the right to **North Birdseye Lookout,** where there is a view of Grandpa Knob and the Adirondacks. The main trail then continues a few more feet to **West Birdseye Lookouts (1.7 m.).** From the Lookouts, the trail quickly completes the summit loop, turns to the right, and retraces its route to **North Peak Junction (1.8 m.).** Here the hiker may either follow other trails south along the ridge or return to the Base Lodge via the North Peak Trail.

SUMMARY: Base Lodge to North Peak and return, 3.4 m.; elevation gained, 1250 ft.; 2¼ hr. round trip.

Butterfly Trail

Taking its name from its staggered figure-eight routing, this trail consists of a double loop linking two views on the west side of the ridge with two lookouts on the east side. Either loop or both may be used as longer but more interesting alternate routing to Castle Peak. From **North Peak Junction (0.0 m.),** the Butterfly Trail and the coinciding Castle Peak Trail follow a woods road south on easy grades around the west slope of Second Peak to a trail junction (0.1 m.), where the Castle Peak Trail takes the left fork. The Butterfly Trail diverges to the right, soon descends westerly into a shallow sag, and then descends very gradually southerly to **Betsey's Balcony (0.2 m.),** where there is an excellent view to the west. After swinging to the left and making a brief climb, the trail continues south with little change of elevation to a spur junction (0.3 m.). To the right via a spur it is about 50 feet to **Sangamon Ledge** and another vista.

From the Sangamon Ledge spur junction, the trail turns sharply left, following an old woods road uphill a short distance before diverging to the left and following a pleasant hogback to the end of the west loop and a crossing of the **Castle Peak Trail (0.4 m.).** To the left via Castle

Peak Trail it is slightly more than 0.1 m. back to North Peak
Junction. To the right it is 0.7 m. to the summit of Castle
Peak. From the trail crossing, the east loop of the Butterfly
Trail climbs easily onto the south slope of Second Peak and
then continues to a spur on the right (0.5 m.) which leads
a few feet to **Herrick Window,** a massive rock outcrop pro-
viding an imposing view of Herrick Mountain and Ben's
Slide, located on its north face.

From Herrick Window the trail turns sharply to the left,
makes a brief steep descent, and then descends more
gradually to a trail junction (0.6 m.). To the left, a spur loop
leads 200 feet to the upper end of the **East Parapet,** one
of several sheer cliffs characteristic of the east flank of the
ridge. After following East Parapet for a short distance, the
loop trail turns sharply right and quickly returns to the main
trail, which bears to the southwest and soon descends to
a woods road. A few feet beyond is a junction with the **Castle
Peak Trail (0.7 m.),** which leaves on the left for that summit. The Butterfly Trail continues straight ahead on an easy
uphill grade to the junction of the west and east loops (0.9
m.), from which point it continues to **North Peak Junction
(1.1 m.).**

SUMMARY: Complete circuit, 1.1 m.; 100 ft. ascent; 40
minutes travel.

Castle Peak Trail

Leaving **North Peak Junction (0.0 m.)** with the coinciding
Butterfly Trail, the Castle Peak Trail follows a woods road
south on easy grades around the west shoulder of Second
Peak. Reaching a junction (0.1 m.), the trail leaves the Butterfly Trail and takes the west fork, continuing gradually
uphill. Passing through the junction of the west and east
loops of the Butterfly Trail (0.2 m.), the Castle Peak Trail
descends easily to the south and southeast along the road
to a final junction with the east loop of the **Butterfly Trail
(0.3 m.),** which continues straight ahead.

Turning sharply right off the road at the junction, the
Castle Peak Trail trends southerly and ascends gradually
along the east flank of the ridge before swinging to the right
(0.4 m.) and climbing somewhat more steeply. Soon beginning a much stiffer climb, with several twists and turns,
the trail continues into an overgrown clearing where it turns
sharply to the right (0.6 m.). At this point there are obscured
views through the trees of the Rutland area and Killington

Peak. Continuing in the open for some distance, the trail then returns to the woods, passes just east of the north summit of Castle Peak, and enters a very shallow sag (0.7 m.). From the sag, the trail ascends easily to the south summit of **Castle Peak (0.8 m.)**, where there is a tunnel view to the west and limited views through the trees to the east and northeast.

From the summit of Castle Peak, the trail descends about 200 feet to the east and south lookouts at **Hawk Ledge**, named for the numerous hawks to be seen soaring above Bird Brook valley. The view to the south is dominated by Herrick Mountain and the rugged dome of Bird Mountain. Because the latter peak is the nesting area for several species of hawks it is strongly recommended that no attempt be made to cross over that summit.

SUMMARY: North Peak Junction to Hawk Ledge, 0.8 m.; 350 ft. ascent; ¾ hr.

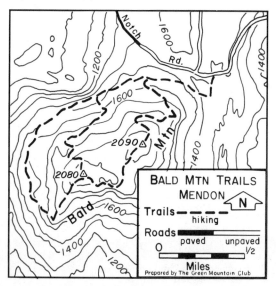

Bald Mountain

Occupying most of the Aitken State Forest in the town of Mendon (see USGS Rutland), the mountain has twin summits and several excellent lookouts which are linked by a blue-blazed trail maintained by the Department of Forests, Parks and Recreation.

From South Main St. in Rutland (US 7), south of the park, follow Killington Ave. east to a junction with Town Line Rd. From the junction (0.0 m.), follow Town Line Rd. south. Turn left at the next fork (0.6 m.) and follow Notch Rd. uphill beyond the end of pavement. Continue straight ahead at the next junction (1.8 m.) to the camp gate on the left (2.0 m.). Limited roadside parking is available just beyond the gate entrance to Tamarack Notch Camp.

From Notch Rd., a few yards west of the camp gate and a brook (0.0 m.), the trail descends gradually to the south on a firewood access road beside the brook. Soon turning to the right after crossing another small brook (0.1 m.), watch for blue blazes on the right. The trail then climbs to a junction (0.4 m.) where alternate routing begins. Turning to the left and soon reversing direction, the main route ascends to a lookout (0.7 m.), where there are views of Pico Peak, its neighbors, and the more distant Okemo Mt.

From the lookout, the trail slabs around a shoulder of the ridge and then ascends steadily to a second lookout (1.1 m.), where there are similar but more extensive views. The trail then continues with little change in elevation to the wooded **north summit (1.2 m.).** Soon turning sharply to the left, the trail descends steadily for a short distance and then continues on easy grades through a shallow sag, staying to the left of a marshy area. The trail then continues to a rock lookout (1.5 m.), where there are views of the Cold River valley.

From the lookout, the trail follows up and down routing past limited views, passes through a rocky ravine, and then ascends to a junction in an open area on the **south summit (1.8 m.),** where there are limited views to the south. Here the hiker must decide whether to take the shorter route back to Notch Rd. via the trail to the right or to complete the longer loop via the trail to the left.

To the right, the shorter trail continues a short distance to **Rutland Lookout** (1.9 m.), where there is a good view of Rutland and the Otter Creek valley to the north. The trail then descends steadily at first and then more moderately to rejoin the main trail (2.4 m.). Turning to the right, trends easterly through the woods and eventually returns to the starting point on **Notch Rd. (3.4 m.)**.

From the south summit junction (1.8 m.), the main trail turns to the left and descends mostly in the open to **Red Rocks Vista** (2.2 m.), where there are wide views to the south, east, and west of the Coolidge Range, Dorset Peak, and the Otter Creek valley.

From the lookout, the trail turns sharply to the right, enters the woods, and descends steeply at first and then more easily. Bearing to the right on an old woods road (2.4 m.), the trail follows easy up and down grades to the north. After reaching a much better woods road (2.7 m.), there soon begins a steady descent to a junction on the right with the previously mentioned loop cutoff (3.2 m.), which leads uphill for 0.6 m. to Rutland Lookout and the upper junction with the main trail.

From the junction, the trail follows the road downhill for a short distance and then turns sharply to the right and enters the woods. Gradually swinging to the east and for the most part descending on easy grades, the trail reaches a junction on the right, which completes the loop, (3.7 m.) and then retraces its route back to **Notch Rd. (4.1 m.)**.

SUMMARY: Complete loop via Red Rocks Vista, 4.1 m.; 750 ft. ascent, 3 hr. (Rev. 3 hr.).

LEAVE NOTHING BUT FOOTPRINTS!

Shrewsbury Peak

Located in the northeast corner of the town of Shrewsbury (see USGS Killington Peak), the summit area offers good views to the east, south, and west. The blue-blazed trail to both the summit and the Long Trail beyond begins at the former Northam Picnic Area, located on the north side of the gravel CCC Road, 2.7 m. from North Shrewsbury and 3.3 m. west of Vt. 100, south of the Woodward Reservoir.

From the parking lot (0.0 m.), the trail swings to the left and follows easy grades to a well (unsafe water), where it swings to the right and ascends steadily past a log leanto (0.2 m.). Passing a short distance east of the summit of **Russell Hill**, the trail then descends into a rocky sag (0.5 m.).

After climbing on easy grades for some distance, the trail begins a steeper ascent (1.0 m.), approaches the west boundary of the Coolidge State Forest (1.5 m.), and then begins a steady, winding climb through dense balsam fir to the **south summit (1.8 m.).** From the several rocky outlooks on the wooded summit (elev. 3720 ft.), there are views to the southeast of Mt. Ascutney, Mt. Kearsarge, and Mt. Monadnock; and to the south of Ludlow Mt., Bromley Mt. and Stratton Mt.

From the south summit, the trail descends into a shallow sag, where the blue-blazed **Black Swamp Trail** departs on the right **(1.9 m.).**

The **Black Swamp Trail** descends 0.3 m. to a spring and **Shrewsbury Peak Shelter**, a log leanto built by the Civilian Conservation Corps. From the shelter the trail descends another 0.9 m. to the end of the Black Swamp Road. From this point it is 2.3 m. to the Northam Picnic Area via the Black Swamp and CCC roads.

A short distance beyond the sag, and just to the right of the Shrewsbury Peak Trail, is the slightly lower **north peak (2.1 m.).** Beyond the north summit, the trail continues for 1.7 m. to the **Long Trail**, from which point it is 1.3 m. north to the summit of **Killington Peak.** A planned relocation of the Long Trail may result in a somewhat longer route.

SUMMARY: Picnic area to summit, 1.8 m.; 1500 ft. ascent; 1¾ hr. (Rev. 1 hr.).

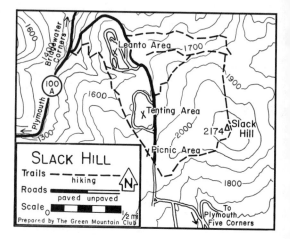

Coolidge State Forest

The hiking trails in Calvin Coolidge State Forest provide several loop hike possibilities, including a 6.4 m. trip that passes near the summit of Slack Hill. The paved access road to the area leaves the east side of Vt. 100A, 4.3 m. south of Bridgewater Corners and 2.7 m. north of Plymouth Union. From the highway, travel 0.9 m. uphill to the contact station. Marked with blue blazes, the trail around the summit begins at the area's contact station.

From the **contact station (0.0 m.)**, the trail ascends easily in an easterly direction. After turning to the right (0.4 m.), the trail climbs steeply to a junction on the right with a blue-blazed trail that descends 0.3 m. to the camp road just above the contact station. Turning left at the junction, the Slack Hill Trail follows gradual up and down grades to another junction (0.8 m.) where there is a sign for Blueberry Leanto.

The trail turns left at this junction, passes an old cellar hole and in about 200 ft. reaches an abandoned town road. The trail turns left again and descends, shortly reaching a cleared area where a new forest highway will be constructed. There is a sharp right turn indicated by an arrow followed by a fairly steep descent past another open area. The road levels out and continues to a paved campground road (1.9 m.), which leads left 0.3 m. to the contact station.

The trail follows the campground access road right toward Vt. 100A. Just above the state highway on the left is a wooden bridge leading to a **picnic pavilion (2.5 m.).** Between the bridge and the access road the blue-blazed trail leads steeply uphill. Shortly the grade lessens and the trail traverses an old woods road. After crossing a small power line (2.9 m.), the trail turns sharply left and reaches a junction where the power line again crosses the trail (3.1 m.). Straight ahead a short trail leads to the leanto loop road and back to the contact station, 0.2 m. from the trail junction.

The trail makes a sharp right turn at the junction and drops steeply downhill through a hemlock grove. At the bottom of the hill the trail crosses a brook then continues uphill at a more moderate grade to another junction (3.5 m.). The trail to the left leads to the tenting area.

Continuing straight at this junction, the route winds steadily uphill and passes very near an orange boundary marker before coming out at the **upper picnic pavilion (3.9 m.).** The trail goes straight through the pavilion and comes out on the park road (4.0 m.).

The Slack Hill Trail (sign) enters the woods just to the right of the road crossing and passes through a stand of tall eastern white pines. Soon entering an open sugar maple forest, the path gently winds uphill to another junction (4.9 m.). The trail turns left here and skirts **Slack Hill**, passing a mixed conifer/hardwood forest on the uphill side. Descending fairly steeply, the trail, enters a northern hardwood forest of beech, birch and maple. After passing through a stone wall, the trail reaches another junction (5.6 m.). The loop is now complete, as this is the junction with the Blueberry Leanto sign.

The return route turns left and follows easy grades to the first junction (5.9 m.). Taking the left fork, the trail winds gradually downhill until it reaches the paved park road (6.2 m.). The route follows the road right to the **contact station (6.4 m.).**

Quechee Gorge Trail

Located in the town of Hartford, Quechee Gorge (USGS Quechee) is a part of the Quechee Recreation Area, owned by the Army Corps of Engineers as part of the North Hartland Dam flood control basin and operated by the Vermont

Department of Forests, Parks and Recreation. The blue-blazed loop trail begins in the central clearing of the camping area, located on the south side of US 4, about half way between Woodstock and White River Jct. There is a day use fee charged to enter the park.

From the south side of the central clearing, the trail enters mature pine and hemlock woods at a woodshed (0.0 m.). After trending southerly on level ground, the trail turns sharply to the right (0.2 m.) and makes a steep descent into a gully. Near the bottom of the gully, another blue-blazed trail enters from the right; keep left at the junction. The trail then climbs over a low ridge, and then descends to cross a small stream on a log bridge (0.3 m.). Following meandering routing on easy up and down grades, the trail crosses another brook (0.4 m.), swings to the left onto a grassy road (0.5 m.), and continues to a junction with a dirt road on the east bank of the Ottauquechee River (0.6 m.), at the lower end of the gorge. To the left, the road follows the river downstream for some distance.

Turning to the right, the trail follows the road upstream along the increasingly higher walls of the narrow gorge. Several spurs to the left offer closer views. Coming in sight of the US 4 bridge, the trail reaches a junction on the right (0.8 m.).

Straight ahead, the road climbs steadily and soon passes under the bridge. Some 165 ft. above the water, the bridge was built in 1911 for the Woodstock Railroad (1875-1933) to replace its original Howe Truss bridge of wood timbers and iron. With the abandonment of the railroad, the bridge and the roadbed in this area became part of US 4. The story of the Woodstock Railroad, of which some of the structures and roadbed are still extant, is told in Mead's *Over the Hills to Woodstock*.

To the north of the bridge, a road leads a short distance to another overlook of the gorge.

From the junction south of the bridge (0.8 m.), the trail turns to the right and follows easy up and down grades parallel to and below the highway. Soon after swinging first left and then right (0.9 m.), the trail makes a short steep climb to the camping area at Site # 16 (1.0 m.) and then returns to the starting point of the loop (1.1 m.).

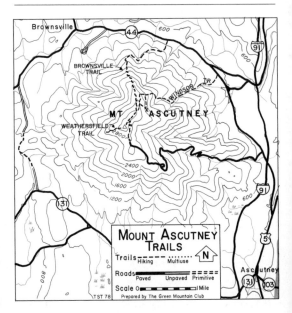

MOUNT ASCUTNEY

A monadnock whose quartz syenite rock has withstood the erosion and glaciation which has worn away the softer rocks of the surrounding Piedmont peneplane, Mt. Ascutney (3150 ft.) is the dominant physical feature of southeastern Vermont. Located in the towns of Windsor and West Windsor (see USGS Claremont), the mountain apparently derives its name from the Indian words "Cas-Cad-Nac" or "Mahps-Cad-Na," meaning "mountain of the rocky summit."

Ascutney State Park (camping facilities, picnic sites) is located on the east slope of the mountain and is reached by a paved road between US 5, north of Ascutney, and Vt. 44, east of Brownsville. From the park entrance, a paved road ascends for about 4 m. to a parking area and lookout located about ¾ m. below the summit.

The trail system is maintained by the Ascutney Trails Association, which has been actively engaged since 1967 in restoration and improvement of these historic trails. Detailed trail data and interesting background information about the mountain's history and features are contained in the ATA's *Guide to the Trails of Ascutney Mountain,* available from the ATA and Windsor area stores.

Windsor Trail

Marked with white blazes, the trail begins on the paved road between US 5, Ascutney State Park, and Vt. 44. The junction is located 0.2 m. south of Vt. 44 and 1.7 m. north of the state park entrance. Parking is permitted along the edge of the field.

From the paved road (0.0 m.), the trail follows the southern boundary of an open field. Beyond the upper end of the field the trail passes through birches and pines and soon enters the woods. The trail then begins an increasingly steep climb on a wide woods road to a spur on the left (0.8 m.), which leads a short distance to **Gerry's Falls** on Mountain Brook.

Soon crossing the right fork of the brook (0.9 m.), the trail follows the left fork upstream a short distance before swinging to the right and slabbing westerly to recross the right fork (1.1 m.). The trail then continues over and around a low shoulder of the mountain to **Half Way Spring (1.5 m.),** where there is a choice of routes of about equal length. Straight ahead, the alternate route continues to a spring and **Log Shelter (1.6 m.),** built in 1968 by the Ascutney Trails Association. Turning to the right, the alternate route soon rejoins the main trail.

From Half Way Spring, the main trail turns sharply to the left and ascends steeply to the south to a junction with the **Blood Rock Trail (1.6 m.).**

Climbing steeply, this blue-blazed trail reaches **Blood Rock,** where there are good views to the north, in about ¼ m. The trail then swings to the west to rejoin the **Windsor Trail (0.5 m.).**

Turning to the right at the Blood Rock Trail junction, the Windsor Trail soon rejoins the alternate route from the shelter (1.7 m.) and begins a steady zig-zag climb past the upper end of the **Blood Rock Trail (1.9 m.)** to a spur on the left (2.3 m.) leading to a view of the Connecticut River valley. A short distance beyond, the trail is joined from the right by the **Brownsville Trail,** with which it continues to an open area and the site of the **Stone Hut (2.4 m.).** To the left, a trail descends 0.7 m. to the summit road parking lot. To the right, a short spur leads to **Brownsville Rock,** where there are extensive views of much of the Green Mountain range. From the Stone Hut site, the trail continues through the woods to the **summit (2.6 m.).**

From the old fire tower on the summit there are extensive views of the White Mountains, Green Mountains, Berkshires and Taconics.

SUMMARY: Road to summit, 2.6 m.; 2500 ft. ascent; 2½ hr. (Rev. 1¼ hr.).

Brownsville Trail

Marked with white blazes, the trail begins opposite a brick house on Vt. 44, 1.2 m. east of the Mt. Ascutney Ski area, 2.8 m. north of Ascutney State Park, and 1.2 m. north of the beginning of the Windsor Trail. Parking is available in the field above the highway.

From the highway (0.0 m.), the trail runs to the right outside a fence enclosing a pasture. It soon enters the woods and climbs steeply to an old road which leads right to the former **Norcross granite quarry (1.1 m.),** one of four which operated at various times in the area.

Beyond the grout pile, the trail turns sharply to the left and climbs steeply to a spur leading a short distance to a lookout with views to the north (1.3 m.). Climbing steadily through the woods, the trail eventually approaches a ski trail (1.6 m.). Here the trail swings sharply to the left and climbs on switchbacks to a lookout (2.0 m.), where there is a view to the east. The trail then continues on easy grades to the summit (2660 ft.) of **North Peak (2.3 m.).** Continuing on easy grades for some distance, the trail then resumes a steep climb via switchbacks to a junction with the **Windsor Trail (2.9 m.).** A short distance beyond, the trail reaches the Stone Hut site (3.0 m.), from which point it is 0.2 m. to the **summit (3.2 m.).**

SUMMARY: Vt. 44 to summit, 3.2 m.; 2400 ft. ascent; 3 hr. (Rev. 1¾ hr.).

Summit Trail

Unblazed but obvious, the trail begins at the end of the automobile road. From the parking area (0.0 m.), the trail ascends gradually to a junction (0.4 m.) marking the beginning of alternate routes of equal length, via the Slot to the right or the Slab to the left. Taking the left fork, the trail makes a winding ascent to the ruins of the Stone Hut, where the alternate route rejoins (0.7 m.). Turning to the left, the route continues to the summit via the white-blazed Windsor Trail (0.9 m.).

SUMMARY: Parking area to summit, 0.9 m.; 350 ft. ascent; ¾ hr. (Rev. ½ hr.).

Weathersfield Trail

This route formerly provided access to the summit of the mountain from the south, but the lower portion of the trail is closed and should not be used. However, the upper portion provides access to fine views at Gus's Lookout and is described here.

From the **summit (0.0 m.)**, the Weathersfield Trail makes a winding descent to a spur trail on the right, which leads a few hundred feet to a fine view from **West Peak (0.4 m.)**. A short distance beyond is a spur to **West Peak Spring (0.5 m.)**. The trail continues its steady descent to **Gus's Lookout (0.6 m.)**, where there is an excellent view of the Connecticut River valley. The lookout is named for Augustus Aldrich, a well known hiking figure who in 1974 died on Mt. Katahdin at age 86.

The trail is closed below this point and should be avoided.

Carry it out! Bring some plastic litter bags and carry out unburnable trash. Some areas are heavily used. Help keep them attractive for others to enjoy.

The Pinnacle

Located in Wilgus State Park (camping area, picnic area), this low hill offers good views of the Connecticut River and the New Hampshire hills to the east. The blue-blazed loop trail begins on US 5, opposite the entrance to the park, 1.1 m. south of Vt. 12 and Vt. 131 in Ascutney village. Parking arrangements should be made with the park manager.

From the highway (0.0 m.), the trail climbs a bank and swings to the left, following a pleasant woods road on easy grades. Eventually turning to the right off the old road (0.3 m.), the trail climbs to a lookout just below the wooded summit (0.5 m.).

From the lookout, the trail passes over the summit (elev. 425 ft.) and makes a steep and winding descent through the woods to the highway (0.9 m.), ¼ m. north of the starting point.

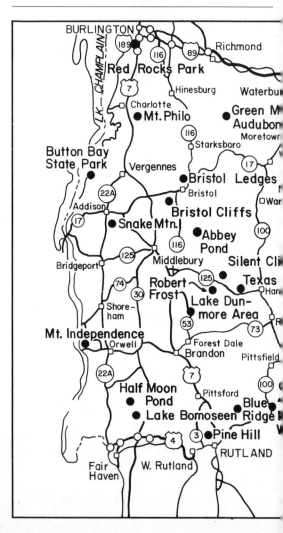

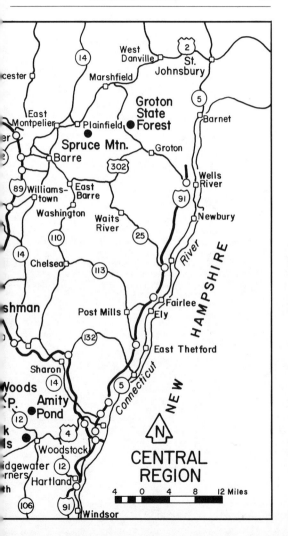

CENTRAL REGION

The Central Region contains portions of five of Vermont's physiographic provinces. All of Addison and Orleans Counties, and parts of Rutland, Windsor, Chittenden, Washington, Caledonia, and Essex Counties are within this region.

The Taconic Mountains and Valley of Vermont occupy a small part of the southern part of the region, and give way to the Champlain Lowlands north of Rutland. For the most part the Lake Champlain valley is gently rolling country, but a number of steep escarpments and an intermittent series of high hills along or near the shore stand out as prominent landmarks.

The central part of the region is dominated by the Green Mountains, which become organized into well defined ranges north of Sherburne Pass. The First, or Front Range consists primarily of the Hogback Mountains in the Bristol-Monkton area. The Second, or Main Range lies somewhat further to the east. The Long Trail generally follows the ridgeline of the Main Range, passing over numerous peaks 3000 feet or more in elevation. Several scenic gaps make prominent breaks in the otherwise generally even skyline of the Main Range. Still further east is the Third Range and its foothills. Bounded on the west by the Mad River valley, the range extends northward to the Winooski River.

The Vermont Piedmont occupies the area east of the Third Range. The piedmont reaches its greatest width in the St. Johnsbury area.

WINTER TRAIL USE

The Green Mountains abound with opportunities for the winter trail user, but the terrain is rugged and weather conditions can be downright hazardous. With proper clothing, equipment, know-how, and preparation, however, a winter outing can be an exhilarating experience.

Hikers planning a winter trip should note:

—At higher elevations, deep snow and snow-laden branches may completely obscure all signs of the trail.

—If you are not an experienced winter hiker, it is best to confine your initial trips to day hikes in areas you are already familiar with from summer use.

—Daylight hours are short in the winter, and darkness may come suddenly. Carry a flashlight.

—Rain in the winter is not uncommon. Be prepared for it.

—Stay alert to the dangers of hypothermia and frostbite. Know the signs and how to treat them before you set out.

—For safety reasons, keep group size between four and ten people.

—Winter trail users planning to stay out overnight must be prepared to keep warm and sheltered with nothing more than the equipment they carry.

—Winter conditions do not necessarily coincide with the calendar. Severe winter weather may be encountered at higher elevations anytime during the fall. In the spring, lower elevation trails may be free of snow, but at higher elevations lingering snow creates very muddy trail conditions.

EMERGENCIES
In case of an emergency on the trail, contact the Vermont State Police.

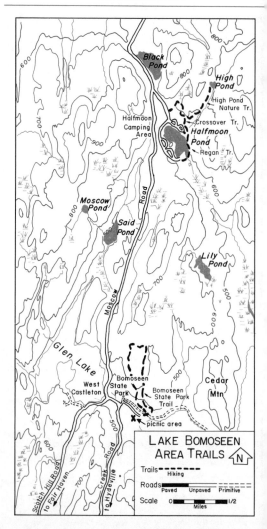

Black Pond

High Pond

High Pond Nature Tr.

Halfmoon Camping Area

Crossover Tr.

Halfmoon Pond

Regan Tr.

Moscow Pond

Said Pond

Lily Pond

Moscow Road

Glen Lake

Bomoseen State Park

West Castleton

Bomoseen State Park Trail

Cedar Mtn

picnic area

Scotch Hill Road

to Fair Haven

Creek Road

to Hydeville

LAKE BOMOSEEN AREA TRAILS

N

Trails — — — —
        Hiking

Roads ———— — — — — —
      Paved   Unpaved   Primitive

Scale 0 ————————— 1/2
              Miles

Half Moon Pond

Part of Bomoseen State Park, the **Half Moon Pond** area (camping only) is reached by following the unpaved Moscow (or Regan) Road north from Bomoseen State Park for about 3 m. From Vt. 30, about 7½ m. north of US 4 at the Castleton Corners exit, the area is reached by following a paved road west for about 2 m. and then following an unpaved road south for about 1½ m.

The blue-blazed **High Pond Nature Trail** leaves the north side of the camp road about half way between the contact station and the camping area. Ascending easily on a winding woods road, the trail passes a junction on the right with the **Crossover Trail** (about ⅓ m.). Soon crossing onto private property, the trail continues for about ½ m. to tiny **High Pond.**

The **Crossover Trail** (blue-blazed) leaves the **High Pond Nature Trail** about ⅓ m. from the camp road and descends to the south for some distance. After climbing to high ground overlooking the pond, the trail descends to the shore and continues to a junction with the **Regan Trail** and the camp road at the south end of the pond. Total distance is about ½ m.

About ⅓ m. long, the blue-blazed **Regan Trail** begins at the south end of the pond near the end of the camp road at a junction with the **Crossover Trail.** After continuing for some distance through pine woods, the trail descends through old fields to a public road, ¾ m. south of the camp entrance.

Bomoseen State Park

Located on the west shore of **Lake Bomoseen** (see USGS Bomoseen), Bomoseen State Park (campground, picnic area) is reached by following a paved road north from Vt. 4A in Hydeville for 4 m. or by following the paved Scotch Hill Road north for 4½ m. from Exit 3 of US 4 in Fair Haven.

A blue-blazed trail, part of which also serves as a nature trail, begins and ends at the far end of the picnic area parking lot. About 1½ m. long, the trail crests a low hill, where there is a good view to the west of **Glen Lake,** and then descends past several views of **Lake Bomoseen.** A free map and nature trail guide is available at the park, where a naturalist is on duty in season.

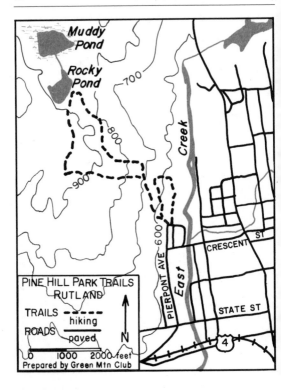

Prepared by Green Mtn Club

Pine Hill Park

Maintained by the City of Rutland Recreation Department, this blue-blazed trail begins and ends at the hockey arena in the John J. Giorgetti Memorial Park section of Pine Hill Park, located in the northwest corner of the city.

From State St. (US 4 West), a short distance before it makes a sharp turn to the left at the top of the hill, follow Pierpoint Ave. north past the Northwest School, and continue past Crescent St. onto Fairview Ave. At Oak St. turn right and continue a short distance to the arena on the left, where there is a large parking area.

From the left front of the building (0.0 m.), the unmarked trail goes over a knoll, beyond which the first blue blazes appear. Quickly turning to the left, the trail soon reaches the white-blazed trail to **Rocky Pond (0.1 m.).** Here the trail turns to the right and follows an easy up and down route to a sag (0.4 m.), where it turns to the right and descends along or near a woods road. Just before reaching the ball field, the trail swings to the right again and continues through the woods to its terminus behind the arena (0.8 m.).

Rocky Pond Trail

This white-blazed trail, maintained by the city of Rutland Recreation Department, leaves the **Pine Hill Park Trail** 0.1 m. west of the hockey arena. From the junction (0.0 m.), the trail quickly takes a fork to the right and ascends to the northwest on old skid roads. Soon after swinging to the left from a woods road, which descends a short distance to the Pine Hill Park Trail, the Rocky Pond Trail crosses a stone wall and reaches a power line, where there are views to the south and east (0.3 m.).

From the power line, the trail swings to the left of an old concrete structure and climbs easily through the woods, crosses the old access road to **Rocky Pond** in a shallow sag (0.6 m.), and rises to another power line clearing (0.8 m.). Here there are good views up and down the Otter Creek valley and of the mountains to the east. The trail then follows the power line to the left for a short distance before turning sharply to the right and descending steadily. After crossing the access road in a sag, the trail slabs around the side of a low ridge and makes a final crossing of the access road about 250 ft. from **Rocky Pond (1.1 m.).**

Crossing the road, the trail follows another road past an abandoned picnic area for a short distance. The trail then turns to the right and follows an up and down route through the woods. Recrossing the upper power line (1.4 m.), the trail descends to join a woods road (1.5 m.) and follows its winding route downhill to the lower power line (1.7 m.), where there is a view to the north. The trail then follows the power line uphill to complete a loop at the old concrete structure (1.8 m.), from which point the trail returns to the hockey arena (2.2 m.).

SUMMARY: Arena to Rocky Pond and return, 2.3 m.; 400 ft. ascent; 1½ hr.

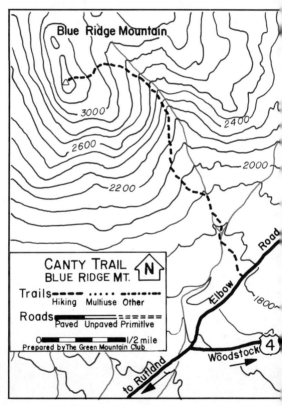

Blue Ridge Mountain

Located in the towns of Mendon and Chittenden (see USGS Chittenden), Blue Ridge Mt. has a number of peaks, the highest and southernmost of which offers good views of Rutland and the Otter Creek valley, Killington Peak and the Coolidge Range, and the White Mountains. The blue-blazed **Canty Trail** to the south summit (elev. 3278 ft.) is maintained by the USFS.

From US 4 opposite the Killington—Pico Motor Inn, about 6 m. east of US 7 in Rutland and 3.7 m. west of the Long Trail at Sherburne Pass, follow Turnpike Road (Elbow Road) northeast uphill to a lane on the left, where there are signs for Tall Timber Camp and Blue Ridge Mt. Roadside parking is extremely limited, but parking arrangements can be made at the Tall Timber Camp office.

From Turnpike Rd. (0.0 m.), the trail follows the lane northwest past the office and buildings of Tall Timber Camp, crosses a small brook, and follows a road into the woods (0.2 m.). Climbing gradually, the trail crosses a large brook on a bridge (0.4 m.). After crossing two smaller streams, the trail bears to the left onto an older woods road (0.9 m.) and begins a steep and rocky climb beside the brook and its numerous cascades. Eventually bearing to the left (1.9 m.), the trail continues on easier grades and continues through pines and birches to a clearing (2.3 m.). Swinging to the right, the trail then ascends to the rocky summit (2.4 m.).

SUMMARY: Turnpike Rd. to summit, 2.4 m.; 1490 ft. ascent; 2 hr. (Rev. 1¼ hr.).

Gifford Woods State Park

Gifford Woods State Park is located on Vt. 100, 0.5 m. north of its junction with U.S. 4 in Sherburne. The **Appalachian Trail** passes through the park on its 2,100 mile passage from Georgia to Maine. In addition, the **Gifford Woods Trail** offers about 0.7 m. of travel in a northern hardwood forest on gentle terrain. The trail starts near the park entrance, circles west of the camping area, crosses the **Appalachian Trail,** and ends at the southern end of the park. Additional information is available at the park.

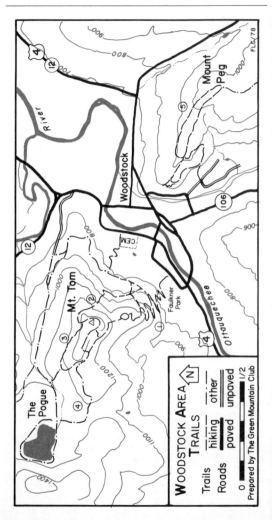

WOODSTOCK TRAILS

From the village of Woodstock, several short trails maintained by the Woodstock Park Commission provide access to Mt. Tom, Mt. Peg, and other points of interest (see USGS Woodstock North, Woodstock South). Additional coinciding or connecting trails are maintained by the Green Mountain Horse Association and the Woodstock Ski Touring Center, both with headquarters in the village. The numbers assigned to the trails in the text correspond to those on the map.

Mount Tom Via Faulkner Trail (1)

The graded pathway, numerous switchbacks, and several park benches along the route make this trail a Vermont rarity. The unblazed but obvious trail begins in Faulkner Park.

From the village green, drive or walk through the covered bridge on Union St. Continue across River St. and take the next left onto Mountain Ave., continuing to Faulkner Park on the right.

Follow the asphalt path along the stone wall which forms the eastern boundary of the park to where the trail enters the woods (0.0 m.), just below a large boulder. The path promptly begins a zig-zag climb on very gradual grades, eventually reaching the yellow-blazed but unsigned **Lower Link Trail (0.5 m.)** on the right. This trail follows easy grades for 0.2 m. to the **North Peak Trail (2).** After some more gradual climbing via switchbacks, the trail reaches a junction on the right with the **Upper Link Trail (1.2 m.)**, which leads 0.2 m. to another junction with the North Peak Trail.

Beyond the Upper Link Trail junction, the trail continues its zig-zag climb to a knoll (1.5 m.), where there are limited views to the south and east. The trail then drops into a shallow sag before beginning a moderately steep climb over the rocks to the end of a carriage road on the south peak (elev. 1240 ft.) of **Mt. Tom (1.6 m.).** Here there are good views to the south of the village and Ludlow Mt. and to the east of the Ottauquechee River. About 125 ft. to the right, at the communication poles, an unmarked and obscure trail (the former Precipice Trail) descends a short distance to a rock lookout, where the views are more impressive.

SUMMARY: Faulkner Park to south peak, 1.6 m.; 550 ft. ascent; 1 hr. (Rev. ¾ hr.).

North Peak Trail (2)

This trail begins on the east side of the River Street Cemetery, reached by following Union St. through the covered bridge and turning right at the first intersection. The entrance is marked by a "Billings Park Trails" sign.

From River St. (0.0 m.), the trail follows an old road, used as a bridle and ski touring trail, on an easy winding ascent. Soon after passing a cabin on the left (0.3 m.), the trail turns sharply left, leaving the old road. Yellow blazes start here. After several hundred feet, there is a junction with the **Lower Link Trail,** which continues straight ahead 0.2 m. to the lower end of the **Faulkner Trail (1).**

Turning sharply to the right at the junction, the trail ascends steadily to another junction (0.4 m.). Turning off to the left here are the yellow-blazed **Middle and Upper Link Trails,** which coincide for about 200 feet before diverging. The **Middle Link Trail** bears left and joins the **Lower Link** 0.1 m. from the **Faulkner Trail.** The **Upper Link Trail** bears right and follows higher ground for 0.2 m. to a junction with the **Faulkner Trail,** 0.4 m. below the south peak.

Turning to the right at the junction, the North Peak Trail descends into a sag, climbs steadily for a short distance, and reaches a junction (0.5 m.) with an unblazed trail entering on the right (which leads to private property). The trail bears sharply left at this junction and then reaches an open rock area offering limited views of the village (0.6 m.). Here the trail turns sharply to the right. Straight ahead is the former Precipice Trail (now closed).

From this turn the trail ascends steadily to a shoulder of south peak (0.7 m.) and continues on easier grades before turning sharply left (0.8 m.) and then reaching a junction on the right with the **Back Loop Trail (3) (0.9 m.).**

Turning left, the trail ascends easily around the north summit of **Mt. Tom,** passes a large boulder on the left where there are views to the south and east, and continues with little change in elevation to a junction on the right with the return leg of the **Back Loop Trail (1.0 m.).** From the junction, the trail descends to the old carriage road (1.1 m.). To the left via the carriage road it is 0.3 m. to the upper end of the **Faulkner Trail.** To the right it is 0.7 m. to the **Pogue.**

SUMMARY: River St. Cemetery to north peak, 1.0 m.; 650 ft. ascent; 1 hr. (Rev. ¾ hr.).

Back Loop Trail (3)

Yellow-blazed, the trail leaves the **North Peak Trail (2)** a short distance below the summit, 0.9 m. from River Street. From the junction (0.0 m.), the trail descends easily through the woods around the back side of the summit ridge to a junction with a woods road (0.3 m.), which descends a short distance to an old road to the **Pogue**. At the junction the trail turns left and ascends through the woods to rejoin the carriage road (0.4 m.). Following the road south for a few yards, the trail then bears to the left and ascends easily through the woods to rejoin the **North Peak Trail (0.8 m.)**.

The Pogue (4)

From the south peak of Mt. Tom (0.0 m.), the unblazed carriage road ascends northwesterly on easy grades. After passing the upper end of the **North Peak Trail (2) (0.3 m.)**, the road bears to the left at a fork with the **Back Loop Trail (3) (0.5 m.)**. Continuing through the woods for some distance, the trail then reaches a large clearing (0.8 m.), where there are extensive views to the west. The trail then descends in the open to a four-way junction (1.0 m.); about 400 feet to the left is the southeast corner of the **Pogue.** A bridle trail circles the small pond, making a loop about ¾ m. long. To the right at the four-way junction, a bridle trail descends along an old road, eventually reaching a junction, where there are trails to Vt. 12 and the River Street Cemetery.

Mount Peg (5)

Located in the southern part of the village, the unblazed, graded path to the summit (elev. 1040 ft.) begins at the intersection of Golf Ave. and Maple St. From the village green, follow South St. (Vt. 106) south to Cross St., follow it to the left across Kedron Brook, turn right onto Golf Ave. at the first intersection, and continue a short distance to the intersection with Maple St.

Just before the Maple St. sign is a three-car parking lot on the left. The trail enters the woods from a driveway behind the parking lot. A sign marks the beginning of the trail.

From the sign (0.0 m.), the trail climbs on switchbacks through the woods. At the first switchback, a partially overgrown abandoned trail enters from the left; keep on the main trail, which turns sharply to the right. At 0.1 m. there is a junction with an alternate trail. Taking the left fork, the main trail climbs northerly for some distance, meets a spur from the left (0.3 m.), and then descends gradually to the south. At 0.4 m. the alternate route rejoins the trail; turn left at this junction. After a short climb there is a junction with a spur on the left from Slayton Terrace. The main trail turns right here and climbs easily southward to a small picnic area on the summit of **Mt. Peg (0.5 m.).**

At the summit, a trail marked initially with blue diamond-shaped markers branches off to the right. This trail passes through woods, crosses a power line, and then reaches the lower end of an old field. Turning left, the trail ascends steadily in the open past extensive views east, north, and west. After reaching the woods on the ridge (0.4 m.), the trail continues for some distance to the Woodstock Country Club.

From the summit loop, the Mt. Peg Trail descends a short distance to complete the loop at the spur from Slayton Ave. (0.6 m.). From this point, either the main trail or the alternate route can be followed back to Golf Ave.

When parking vehicles at trailheads and road junctions, hikers should take special care to avoid obstructing traffic or blocking access to homes, farms, or woodlots. Vandalism can be a problem at some trailhead parking areas, and it may be wiser to leave your car in town, especially if you will be out overnight.

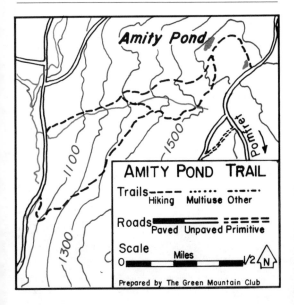

Amity Pond Natural Area

Located in the northwest part of Pomfret, the Amity Pond Natural Area (USGS Woodstock North) consists of woodlands and upland pastures donated to the state for non-motorized outdoor recreation. The area is circled by a loop trail, part of which serves as routing for the **Sky Line Trail**, a cross-country ski trail. The trail is marked with blue and orange markers.

From US 4 in Woodstock, follow Vt. 12 north 1.2 m. to a fork. Turn right onto the South Pomfret road. At the South Pomfret post office (3.2 m.), bear right at the fork and continue through the village of Pomfret to a junction in the hamlet of Hewetts Corners (7.9 m.). At this junction bear right, staying on the paved road. Take the first left onto another paved road at the junction where the I-89 sign is located, and continue to a gravel road on the left (8.3 m.).

Follow this gravel road uphill to a small parking area opposite the entrance to the area on the height of land (10.4 m.).

From the road (0.0 m.), the trail quickly reaches a spur which leads left a short distance to **Amity Pond Shelter.** Taking the right fork, the trail ascends first through a wooded area and then in the open to the height of land, where there are views of Mt. Ascutney, Killington Peak, and Pico Peak. Turning to the south, the trail then passes tiny **Amity Pond (0.2 m.),** named to commemorate the lifelong friendship of two area women who met frequently at this spot.

After passing the pond the trail descends, still in the open. Just beyond the crest of the hill the trail diverges (0.3 m.). This junction is very easy to miss. Following the right fork, the trail descends through the woods to a spur trail, which joins the main trail at a very sharp angle on the left.

Hikers who desire a shorter walk may take this route, which cuts across to the return leg of the Amity Pond Trail. The cutoff trail follows an old woods road for a short distance, turns right, and crosses a stream on a plank bridge. After ascending through the woods, the trail crosses a power line and joins the return leg of the main trail.

A short distance past the cutoff spur, the Amity Pond Trail reaches another spur leading left a short distance to **Sugar Arch Shelter.** Just beyond the spur the trail passes through a small clearing (0.7 m.), descends through the woods and crosses a power line (0.8 m.). After descending steadily on an abandoned road, the trail enters a large field (0.9 m.) by two apple trees. Continuing straight across the field, the trail reaches **Broad Brook Road** and turns left.

Immediately after crossing Broad Brook on a concrete bridge (1.2 m.) the trail crosses the stream on rocks and follows a woods road to the right along **Broad Brook.** Shortly, the trail makes a sharp left turn (1.3 m.), begins a winding climb, and crosses a brook (1.5 m.). After passing through an old moss covered stone wall (1.8 m.), the trail makes another sharp left where the trail parallels the orange marked boundary line.

The Amity Pond Trail passes the cutoff to Sugar Arch Shelter on the left (2.0 m.), crosses a powerline (2.2 m.), and drops down to a brook crossing (2.3 m.). After climbing steadily for a short distance the trail leaves the woods and continues uphill through the field. After about 100 ft.

the trail rejoins the access route, and the loop is completed. Turning right, the trail passes **Amity Pond** and returns to the parking area (2.7 m.).

Mount Independence

Occupying a peninsula on the east shore of Lake Champlain in the town of Orwell, this low hill (elev. 306 ft.) has a commanding view of the narrow lake and nearby Fort Ticonderoga (see USGS Ticonderoga). For this reason, it was fortified by the Americans to bolster the weak defenses of Fort Ticonderoga followings its capture by the Green Mountain Boys in 1775.

A strong show of force at Independence and Ticonderoga plus the lateness of the season prompted the British to give up their plans for recapturing the fort in late 1776. The following spring, however, they made the American positions untenable by laboriously hauling their heavy artillery to the summit of Mt. Defiance, a craggy hill on the west shore which the Americans had thought inaccessible. The hasty retreat from Fort Ticonderoga and Mt. Independence gave the British control of the lake again and set the stage for the battles of Hubbardton, Bennington, and Saratoga.

Most of the Mt. Independence area is owned by the Fort Ticonderoga Association and the State of Vermont and is open to the public between Memorial Day and mid-October. Three scenic foot trails leading past the marked sites of the well preserved remains of the fortifications begin north of the visitor's center and museum. A brochure containing a trail map and a history of the area is available at the site or from the Vermont Division for Historic Preservation in Montpelier.

Mt. Independence is reached by following Vt. 73 and Vt. 73A west from Vt. 22A, near Orwell, for about 3½ m. and then following a road to the right for about 1¾ m.

Beginning at the trail information outpost, the **Orange Trail** (2.5 m.) crosses the highest point of the mountain and continues nearly to the tip of the peninsula, where a short spur loops to the shore and back. The trail then returns to the starting point via parallel routing to the east.

Beginning and ending at the trail information outpost, the **Red Trail** (0.6 m.), makes a loop to the west, where there are views of **Mt. Defiance** and **Fort Ticonderoga.**

Beginning and ending at the trail information outpost, the **White Trail** (0.8 m.) makes a loop to the east side.

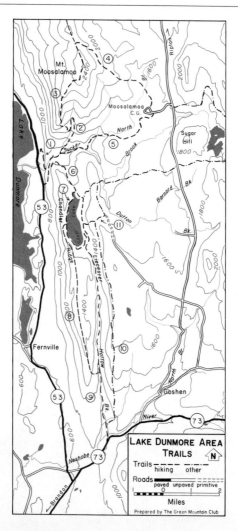

LAKE DUNMORE AREA
TRAILS   N

Trails - - - -
        hiking   other
Roads
        paved unpaved primitive

Miles

Prepared by The Green Mountain Club

LAKE DUNMORE AREA

Located in the Green Mountain National Forest and Branbury State Park, this network of trails links the state park with the USFS Falls of Lana Picnic Area, Silver Lake Recreation Area (picnic area, campground), and Moosalamoo Campground. **Silver Lake, Rattlesnake Cliffs,** and the **Falls of Lana** are some of the natural highlights in this area (see USGS East Middlebury).

Branbury State Park Nature Trail

Located on the east side of Lake Dunmore, Branbury State Park (campground, picnic area) is reached by following Vt. 53 north about 6 m. from Vt. 73 at Forest Dale or about 3.5 m. south from US 7, south of Middlebury.

About one third of a mile long, the nature trail begins and ends on the east side of Vt. 53 just beyond a private camp, 0.2 m. north of the park entrance. A nature trail guide is available at the park, where naturalists are on duty during the camping season.

Falls of Lana Trail (1)

In part utilizing the Branbury State Park Nature Trail and the USFS **Silver Lake Trail (6),** the blue-blazed trail begins on the east side of Vt. 53, 0.2 m. north of the park entrance.

From the highway (0.0 m.), the trail makes a winding ascent past several stations of the nature trail to a woods road (0.1 m.). Climbing steeply on the road for a short distance, the trail then turns to the right (0.2 m.) and continues on easy grades to cross a power line (0.3 m.), where there is a good view of **Rattlesnake Point,** the southernmost peak of Mt. Moosalamoo. After crossing a small stream in a wet area, the trail swings to the south and begins a steep and winding climb past several views of lake Dunmore. At 0.5 m. the trail switches back to the left. Here another blue-blazed trail continues straight ahead and then descends 0.2 m. to the camping area and Vt. 53. The trail reaches the **Falls of Lana Picnic Area (0.6 m.)** and is poorly marked from there on. Follow upstream along worn path about 100 yards to a signed trail junction. To the left is the **Rattlesnake Cliffs Trail (2)** which leads to Rattlesnake Point, Mt. Moosalamoo, and the Moosalamoo Campground.

Turning to the right, the Falls of Lana Trail crosses Sucker Brook and follows a woods road downstream to its terminus on the **Silver Lake Trail (6) (0.7 m.).**

The **Falls of Lana** are located a short distance downstream and can be viewed from several unmarked spurs. Here Sucker Brook has carved a deep gorge in the solid rock. When a party, which included General Wool of the U.S. Army, visited the site in 1850, they decided that Sucker Brook Falls was too prosaic a name. During his tour of duty in Mexico, the general had become known as General Llana, the Spanish word for wool. In tribute to the general, the party christened the site the Falls of Lana.

From the junction, the trail descends along the road to Vt. 53 (1.2 m.), from which point it is 0.4 m. north via the highway to the park.

Rattlesnake Cliffs Trail (2)

Completed in 1977 by the Youth Conservation Corps and rebuilt in 1983 by a crew from the Rutland Community Correction Center, this blue-blazed USFS trail begins a loop of 7¾ m. linking the Falls of Lana Picnic Area, Rattlesnake Point, Mt. Moosalamoo, and the Moosalamoo Campground. The trail begins at the **Falls of Lana Picnic Area.**

From the junction (0.0 m.), the trail follows a woods road to a junction on the right with the **North Branch Trail (5) (0.3).** Taking the left fork, the Rattlesnake Cliffs Trail follows a woods road across a small stream. After climbing steadily for some distance, the trail crosses the brook again (0.9 m.) and swings to the south. Slabbing the east slope of the ridge, the trail eventually reaches a junction on the right with the **Oak Ridge Trail (3) (1.5 m.).** Turning left, the trail leads to **Rattlesnake Cliffs (1.6 m.),** where there are spectacular views of Silver Lake and Lake Dunmore.

SUMMARY: Falls of Lana Picnic Area to Rattlesnake Cliffs, 1.6 m.; 870 ft. ascent; 1¼ hr. (Rev. ¾ hr.).

Oak Ridge Trail (3)

From its southern terminus at the **Rattlesnake Cliffs Trail (2) (0.0 m.),** the Oak Ridge Trail follows a ridge north on easy grades past several views to the west and south of Lake

Dunmore, Lake Champlain, and Lake George. Soon after crossing the Keewaydin Trail on a knoll (0.9 m.), the trail dips into a shallow sag and then makes a winding climb to the **middle summit** of **Mt. Moosalamoo (1.2 m.)**. The trail then continues along the ridge to the **north summit** of **Mt. Moosalamoo (1.4 m.)**, where there are good views to the east and south.

From the summit, the trail descends along the ridge to the north and reaches a junction on the right with the **Moosalamoo Trail (4) (1.6 m.)**. Continuing past more good views to the east and west, the trail crosses an old logging road and eventually reaches an old road and a telephone line, which it follows west to a parking area on Vt. 125 (7.1 m.).

SUMMARY: Rattlesnake Cliffs Trail to Vt. 125, 7.1 m.; 1200 ft. ascent; 4¼ hr. (Rev. 4¾ hr.).

Moosalamoo Trail (4)

Linking the **Oak Ridge Trail (3)** with the USFS **Moosalamoo Campground,** this trail departs from the former a short distance north of the summit of Mt. Moosalamoo.

The Moosalamoo Trail leaves the **Oak Ridge Trail** junction **(0.0 m.),** and continues to a right turn (0.2 m.), where it begins a short but steady descent. Continuing more gradually along the east flank of the mountain, the trail reaches an overgrown woods road, where it makes another right turn (0.7 m.). Soon bearing to the left (0.8 m.), the trail descends on easy grades through the woods to the southeast and eventually crosses the north branch of **Voter Brook (1.8 m.).** The trail then climbs around and over a knoll to **Moosalamoo Campground (2.3 m.).** The camping area is located 0.4 m. west of the Ripton-Goshen Road, about 3 m. south of Vt. 125.

SUMMARY: Oak Ridge Trail to Moosalamoo Campground, 2.3 m.; 800 ft. descent; 1 hr. (Rev. 1½ hr.).

North Branch Trail (5)

From **Moosalamoo Campground (0.0 m.),** the North Branch Trail follows easy grades on high ground and eventually makes a short steep descent to cross the north branch of **Voter Brook (1.1 m.).** The trail then follows the brook downstream on high ground past interesting cascades. Crossing the main branch of **Voter Brook (1.3 m.)**, the trail follows the brook downstream on easy up and down grades, passes over a wooded knoll (1.7 m.), and descends to its terminus at the **Rattlesnake Cliffs Trail (2) (2.2 m.)**. Straight ahead it is 0.3 m. to the Falls of Lana Picnic Area.

SUMMARY: Moosalamoo Campground to Rattlesnake Cliffs Trail 2.2 m.; 650 ft. descent; 1 hr. (Rev. 1½ hr.).

Silver Lake Trail (6)

Located in the northeast corner of Leicester, **Silver Lake** and the USFS Silver Lake Recreation Area (picnic area and camping at designated sites only) are reached by an unblazed but obvious trail which begins at a large turnout located on the east side of Vt. 53, 5.5 m. north of Forest Dale.

From the highway (0.0 m.), the trail climbs a short distance to the east and turns to the right onto a good woods road, which soon swings to the north and ascends on easy grades. Passing under the penstock which brings water from Silver Lake to the power plant on Vt. 53 (0.3 m.), the trail continues past unmarked spurs to the **Falls of Lana** and soon reaches a junction (0.5 m.). Straight ahead, the **Falls of Lana Trail (1)** continues a short distance across Sucker Brook to a junction, where there are trails for the picnic area, Branbury State Park, Rattlesnake Point, Mt. Moosalamoo, and Moosalamoo Campground.

Turning to the right, the Silver Lake Trail ascends to the east for a short distance and then resumes its northerly direction (0.6 m.). Following easy grades, the trail passes a beaver meadow to the left (1.2 m.) and ascends to a power line clearing (1.4 m.). After following the power line for a short distance, the trail turns to the right (1.5 m.) and a few feet beyond reaches a junction just below the **Silver Lake dam (1.5 m.)**. To the right is the **Silver Lake Loop Trail (7)**. Ahead, the **Leicester Hollow Trail (9)** leads around the north shore of the lake.

SUMMARY: Vt. 53 to Silver Lake dam, 1.5 m.; 525 ft. ascent; 1 hr. (Rev. ¾ hr.).

Silver Lake Loop Trail (7)

This recently constructed USFS trail, marked with blue blazes but not yet signed, begins just below the dam at the terminus of the **Silver Lake Trail (6)**. From the junction

(0.0 m.), the trail descends to cross the brook just below the dam and then follows the west shore of the lake, occasionally clambering onto the rocky slopes of Chandler Ridge to find room. To the rear, there are frequent views of Mt. Moosalamoo. After crossing a point and a junction with the **Chandler Ridge Trail (8) (0.5 m.)**, the trail crosses a small inlet brook at the southwest corner of the lake (1.3 m.) and continues through the woods to the southeast corner (1.5 m.), crosses an inlet brook on a bridge (1.6 m.), and swings to the north. After following the east shore for a short distance, the trail swings to the right and continues to a junction with the **Leicester Hollow Trail (9) (1.7 m.)**. From the junction it is 0.2 m. to the **Goshen Trail (11)** and 0.8 m. back to the dam, making a total loop distance of 2.5 m.

Chandler Ridge Trail (8)

This blue-blazed USFS trail leaves the **Silver Lake Loop Trail (7)** on the west side of the lake and rises to the height of land. It then proceeds at gentle grades south along Chandler Ridge for 3.5 m. with spectacular views east to the Green Mountains and west to the Champlain Valley and Adirondacks. It terminates at the 0.4 m. mark of the **Leicester Hollow Trail (9)**.

Leicester Hollow Trail (9)

This unblazed but obvious USFS trail begins on Forest Road 40, which leaves the north side of Vt. 73, 0.8 m. east of Vt. 53 at Forest Dale.

From the highway (0.0 m.), the trail soon crosses the **Neshobe River (0.1 m.)** and continues to a junction on the right with the **Ridge Trail (10) (0.3 m.)**. Entering the National Forest a short distance beyond (0.4 m.), the trail passes a junction with the **Chandler Ridge Trail (8)** on the left and ascends northerly on easy grades and eventually makes the first of numerous crossings (0.9 m.) of **Leicester Hollow Brook**. Ascending deeper into the hollow past old rock slides and mossy boulders, the trail passes an attractive gorge and pool on the left (2.9 m.) and continues its gradual climb to a junction (unmarked) with the **Silver Lake Loop Trail (7)** on the left (3.8 m.). The trail then continues past a junction on the right with the **Goshen Trail (11) (4.0 m.)**, and passes several campsite spurs on the left (4.2 m.). After crossing an inlet stream on a bridge, the trail passes through the picnic area and ends at the **Silver Lake Trail (6)** near the dam **(4.6 m.).**

SUMMARY: Vt. 73 to Silver Lake dam, 4.6 m.; 450 ft. ascent; 2½ hr. (Rev. 2¼ hr.).

Ridge Trail (10)

This trail is marked with blue rectangles and generally parallels the **Leicester Hollow Trail (9)** on higher ground to the east. The trail leaves the Leicester Hollow Trail 0.3 m. north of Vt. 73.

From the junction (0.0 m.), the trail ascends to the right on a woods road beside a brook. Turning to the left and crossing the brook (0.3 m.), the trail ascends gradually toward the ridge but never crosses it. Bearing to the left at all junctions and briefly following reddish orange blazes beyond the Glade Trail junction (1.8 m.), the trail eventually reaches a junction with the **Goshen Trail (11) (3.9 m.),** 0.4 m. east of its junction with the Leicester Hollow Trail.

Goshen Trail (11)

Marked with blue blazes, this USFS trail begins at a parking area located at the end of Forest Road 27. From Vt. 73, 1.6 m. east of Forest Dale, follow the Goshen–Ripton road north for 2.3 m. to a cross roads. Turn left onto Forest Road 27 and continue north to the end of the road (4.3 m.) and the parking area.

From the parking area (0.0 m.), the trail crests a low ridge and crosses a power line (0.1 m.). Descending through the woods, the trail reaches a junction on the left with the **Ridge Trail (10) (0.2 m.),** crosses a small stream in a hollow (0.3 m.), and rises to join an old road (0.4 m.). The trail then descends to its terminus at the **Leicester Hollow Trail (9) (0.6 m.).**

**Protect Vermont's Hiking Trails
JOIN THE GMC**

Robert Frost Trail

About 1.0 m. long, this USFS trail begins at a parking area on the south side of Vt. 125, 2.1 m. east of Ripton and 3.8 m. west of Middlebury Gap (see USGS East Middlebury). Along the loop through the woods and old clearings, several of Robert Frost's poems can be enjoyed in appropriate settings. The USFS maintains all of the old fields along this trail with prescribed fire to preserve the scenic open appearance of the area.

Silent Cliff Trail

This blue-blazed USFS trail leaves the Long Trail 0.4 m. north of Vt. 125 at Middlebury Gap and ascends easterly to Silent Cliff, where there is a good view of the Middlebury Gap area (see USGS Bread Loaf).

SUMMARY: Vt. 125 to Silent Cliff, 0.8 m.; 520 ft. ascent; ¾ hr. (Rev. ½ hr.).

Texas Falls Nature Trail

From Vt. 125, 3.2 m. east of Middlebury Gap and 3.1 m. west of Vt. 100 in Hancock, a paved road leads north 0.5 m. to a parking area on the left. From the parking area, a self-guiding nature trail (descriptive folder available at the site) crosses a rustic bridge over **Texas Falls** and follows **Hancock Brook** upstream for 0.3 m. toward the Texas Falls Picnic Area. Bear right just before crossing the paved road at the picnic area to reach the upper section of the nature trail which leads 0.9 m. back to the falls.

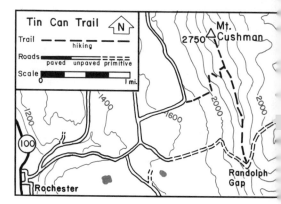

Mount Cushman

Located in the town of Rochester, the summit (USGS Hancock) has a cleared area from which there are good views to the west of the Green Mountains from the Lincoln Range southward to Killington Peak. Limited views are also available from the site of a former fire tower, located on a lesser summit to the south.

The most common approach is via the Tin Can Trail. From the village of Rochester on Vt. 100, turn east at the north end of the common (0.0 m.) and follow the paved Rochester-Bethel Road until it makes a sharp right turn (1.4 m.). Continue straight on North Hollow Road and take the first right (1.6 m.). Follow this narrow gravel road past a field on the right (2.3 m.). At this point the road forks and becomes impassable. Very limited parking is available.

From the end of the public road (0.0 m.), the abandoned **Randolph Gap Road** (left fork) climbs steadily past a fork to the left (0.4 m.) to a junction at the height of land (0.9 m.). Continuing straight ahead, the old road descends 1.2 m. to a public road which leads north for 2.9 m. and then east for 4.5 m. to the village of Randolph.

From the junction, the **Tin Can Trail** turns sharply to the left and follows an old woods road along or near the ridge, ascending for the most part on easy grades. After passing over a knoll (1.5 m.), the trail continues to a clearing and the site of the former fire tower (2.1 m.). Through a gap in the trees there is a limited view to the south.

Just south of the clearing, a well-defined trail descends steeply to the west following a zig-zag routing 0.7 m. to a field and then follows old wheel tracks to a gate and public road at the northwest corner of the field (0.9 m.). Via public roads, it is 1.3 m. south and east to the Randolph Gap Road trailhead.

From the old fire tower clearing, the trail descends into a sag and then climbs along the ridge on an old woods road. Just before reaching the summit, the trail bears to the left and continues a short distance to a cleared area (2.6 m.).

SUMMARY: End of public road to summit 2.6 m.; 1130 ft. ascent; 2 hr. (Rev. 1½ hr.).

Button Bay State Park

Located on Lake Champlain, Button Bay State Park (campground, picnic area, natural area) is reached by following town roads west and south from Vt. 22A, about a half mile south of the traffic light in Vergennes.

There is a short nature trail, the **Champlain Trail,** in the park. A nature trail guide and a pamphlet describing the interesting geology of Button Bay can be obtained at the Button Point Nature Center.

SPRING HIKING DISCOURAGED

The Green Mountain Club discourages hiking during the spring mud season, usually from mid-April to the end of May. Snow lingering at the higher elevations creates very wet and muddy conditions. Hiker's boots do much more damage to wet and muddy trails than when the trails are dry and more stable.

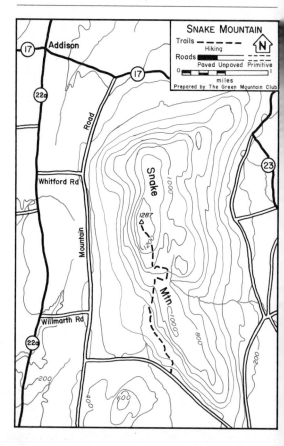

Snake Mountain

Located on the Addison-Weybridge town line (see USGS Port Henry), the summit (elev. 1287 ft.) offers excellent views of the Champlain valley and the Adirondacks. The name derives from the serpentine shape of its long ridge. The equally appropriate name of Grand View Mountain was substituted some time after 1870, when a hotel was established on the summit. The new name, however, lasted only slightly longer than the summit house. Much of the mountain is included in the 999 acre Snake Mountain Wildlife Management Area. However, the summit and the lower end of the trail are on private property.

From Vt. 17, 0.8 m. east of Addison Four Corners and Vt. 22A, follow Mountain Road south past the former start of the trail at Willmarth Road (2.7 m.). Turn left onto Mountain Road Extension at the next fork (3.3 m.) and continue to a woods road on the left (3.9 m.), where the remains of a barn are visible. Limited parking is available opposite the barn.

From the road junction (0.0 m.), the trail follows the woods road north to a junction on the left with the old summit carriage road (0.5 m.). After continuing somewhat more steeply to the north, the trail swings to the east onto the ridge and reaches a junction (0.9 m.). The trail takes the left fork and climbs on easy to moderate grades. After a sharp swing to the left (1.2 m.), the trail soon resumes a northerly direction, bears to the left at a fork in a shallow sag (1.7 m.), and continues to the summit (1.8 m.).

SUMMARY: Road to summit, 1.8 m.; 900 ft. ascent; 1½ hr. (Rev. 1 hr.).

Bristol Ledges

From the ledges on the southwest side of **Hogback Mt.**, there are good views of Bristol village and the lower Champlain valley. The ledges are reached by following an unmarked woods road westerly from the **Bristol Reservoir.**

From Main St. (Vt. 116), a short distance east of the shopping district, turn left onto Mountain St. Then turn right onto Mountain Terr., take the next right turn and continue to the end of the street. Very limited parking is available at the end of the street.

From the end of the street (0.0 m.), the trail follows a winding jeep road easterly to the **Bristol Reservoir (0.3 m.).** Just before reaching the reservoir clearing, a woods road forks to the left and continues straight ahead uphill. Soon turning sharply to the left (0.4 m.), the trail ascends easily in a northerly direction, meets a cutoff spur from the reservoir junction on the left (0.5 m.), and then climbs fairly steadily to the rock ledges (1.0 m.).

Bristol Cliffs Wilderness

Part of the Green Mountain National Forest, the Bristol Cliffs Wilderness consists of over 3700 acres located in the South Mountain area southeast of Bristol (see USGS South Mountain). Permits are not required for entry into the area.

There are no marked trails or established campsites in the Wilderness. However, there are several natural attractions, including the cliffs and jumbled talus slopes for which the area is named. These cliffs rise 1500 ft. above the Champlain Valley and provide a spectacular view of Lake Champlain and the Adirondack Mountains.

For further information, including a map of the area, contact the U.S. Forest Service, Middlebury Ranger District (RD 4, Box 1260, Middlebury, Vt. 05753 or 802-388-4362).

The hiking times in this book are not necessarily those you will or should take. They are calculated with a formula (pg. 22) and are included only to serve as a guide.

Your membership in the GMC supports hiker educational programs

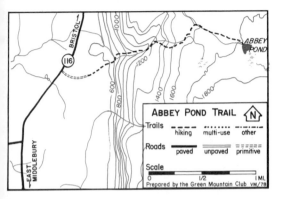

Abbey Pond

Located in the northwest corner of Ripton, this attractive wilderness pond is reached by a blue-blazed USFS trail which follows old woods roads along or near the outlet brook (see USGS South Mountain). From the pond there is an interesting view of the twin peaks of Robert Frost Mt.

Reach the trail by turning east off Vt. 116 4.3 m. north of Vt. 125 in East Middlebury onto a dirt road marked with a U.S. Forest Service trail sign. The dirt road forks immediately; take the right fork. (The two forks rejoin, but flooding in the spring of 1982 washed out both roads and only the right fork has been rebuilt.) Proceed 0.4 m. to an intersection. The trail goes straight ahead from here. Park well off the roads as they are used by gravel trucks.

From the dirt road (0.0 m.), the trail follows an old woods road and crosses the outlet of **Abbey Pond** just below a series of cascades (0.2 m.). Soon swinging to the right and climbing steadily, the trail recrosses the brook (0.6 m.) and bears to the left at a fork (0.9 m.) before continuing on easy grades to a third and final brook crossing (1.2 m.). After bearing away from the brook (1.4 m.), the trail ascends gradually through occasional wet areas to reach the pond near its outlet (1.9 m.).

SUMMARY: Vt. 116 to pond, 1.9 m.; 1160 ft. ascent; 1½ hr. (Rev. 1 hr.).

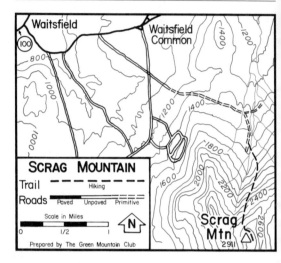

Scrag Mountain

Until recent years the site of a fire lookout tower, the summit (USGS Waitsfield) still offers limited views of the Green Mountains and the White Mountains. Although not maintained for several years, the former lookout's trail from the west is still well defined.

From the village of Waitsfield on Vt. 100, turn east at the yellow brick library (0.0 m.) and cross the covered bridge. Turn left at the next fork (0.4 m.), cross a narrow bridge and continue up a steep hill. Make a right turn (1.1 m.) onto Cross Road and follow it to a four-way intersection (1.8 m.). Continue straight ahead and follow a narrow dirt road east. Pass a driveway on the right (2.9 m.) and take the right fork at the next junction (3.1 m.). Continue uphill and park at a log landing (3.4 m.). The road may not always be passable to this point.

From the log landing (0.0 m.), the trail follows the left fork of the logging road to a large hemlock tree bearing a sign (0.1 m.). Here the trail branches to the left. Gradually swinging to the south and climbing steadily, the trail slabs the ridge, following the remains of the telephone line. At a spur (1.2 m.) leading to water, the trail turns sharply to the left and continues on easier grades to the ridge and the site of the former lookout's cabin (1.4 m.). The trail turns to the south here and continues a short distance to the tower site (1.5 m.), from which point there are limited views.

SUMMARY: Parking area to summit, 1.5 m.; 1350 ft. ascent; 1½ hr. (Rev. ¾ hr.).

Mount Philo

Mount Philo State Park (campground, picnic area) is located east of US 7, about 15 m. south of Burlington and about 9 m. north of Vergennes. From the picnic area, the blue-blazed **Cliff Trail** makes a loop of about ¾ m. around the broad summit area. The loop can be made considerably longer by using either of the two spurs connecting with the loop road around the park.

Some of the finest views available of the Adirondacks and nearly the entire length of **Lake Champlain** can be seen from the north and west ledge lookouts of this 980 ft. high mountain.

Red Rocks Park

The Red Rocks Park trail system consists of several interconnected paths that lead through pleasant pine woods to vantage points on the shore of **Lake Champlain.** The park, trails, and a picnic area are maintained by the City of South Burlington Recreation Department.

From U.S. 7, a few yards south of the Interstate 189 interchange, follow Queen City Park Drive west. After crossing a very narrow bridge across railroad tracks, turn left and continue a short distance to the park entrance. A parking fee is charged from late June to Labor Day, but pedestrians may enter without charge at any time.

Green Mountain Audubon Nature Center

The Green Mountain Audubon Nature Center is located on the west side of the Richmond-Huntington Road, about 5 m. south of Richmond village and about 1 m. north of Huntington village. There is a visitor center with parking on the Sherman Hollow Road about ¼ m. west of the highway.

Owned by the Green Mountain Audubon Society, the Nature Center is a 230 acre sanctuary that includes a working sugarbush and sugarhouse. There is no fee, but contributions are accepted. Green Mountain Audubon also offers a variety of natural history programs for adults and children. Contact the Center (RD 1, Box 189, Richmond, Vt. 05477 or 802-434-3068) for information.

A five mile network of trails, open every day from dawn to dusk, crisscrosses the property. These trails lead to a variety of wildlife habitats and offer views of the neighboring mountains, with Camel's Hump the most spectacular. A trail map is available at the Center.

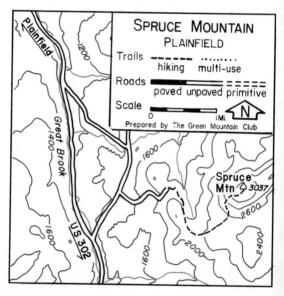

Spruce Mountain

Located in the town of Plainfield (see USGS East Barre), the summit is the site of an abandoned fire tower, from which there is a wide view of north central Vermont and western New Hampshire. The unblazed but obvious trail to the summit is partly located in the L. R. Jones State Forest and partly in Groton State Forest.

From US 302, 1.1 m. east of East Barre, turn north on the Plainfield Springs Road (0.0 m.). After reaching the end of pavement (4.9 m.), continue to a junction on the right with East Hill Road (5.7 m.). Follow East Hill Road uphill, and then turn right onto Spruce Mountain Road (6.5 m.). At the next junction (6.8 m.), turn left and follow the narrow and winding road to a parking area and gate at the start of the trail (7.5 m.).

From the gate (0.0 m.), the trail turns right and follows a wide woods road to the southeast. After an initial brief climb, the trail descends gradually for some distance, offering occasional views of the tower, and then climbs on easy grades. Gradually swinging to the east, the trail reaches the end of the well defined road (1.0 m.). The trail then continues through several wet areas, where former fire tower lookouts have placed stepping stones and fill. After passing two small springs and an obscure snowmobile trail junction on the right, the trail continues a short distance further to cross a small stream (1.3 m.).

Following a northeasterly course in the deep woods, the trail soon begins a moderately steep climb (1.5 m.) past two large boulders (1.6 m.) and then climbs somewhat less steeply over the granite bedrock for some distance. Resuming a steady ascent (1.9 m.), the trail continues through a fern clearing and then continues on easier grades to the summit and the tower (2.2 m.).

SUMMARY: Parking area to summit, 2.2 m.; 1180 ft. ascent; 1¾ hr. (Rev. 1 hr.).

Never underestimate the variability of Vermont weather! Always be prepared for rain and cold.

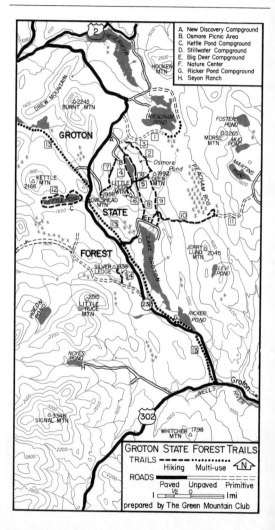

A. New Discovery Campground
B. Osmore Picnic Area
C. Kettle Pond Campground
D. Stillwater Campground
E. Big Deer Campground
F. Nature Center
G. Ricker Pond Campground
H. Seyon Ranch

GROTON STATE FOREST TRAILS

TRAILS ---------- ▪▪▪▪▪▪▪▪▪▪   ⌂ N

    Hiking   Multi-use

ROADS ═══════ ────── ═ ═ ═ ═

    Paved   Unpaved   Primitive

½   0   1mi

prepared by The Green Mountain Club

GROTON STATE FOREST

The largest single piece of state property, Groton State Forest consists of about 26,000 acres in the towns of Groton, Peacham, Marshfield, Orange, and Topsham (see USGS Plainfield, East Barre, Woodsville). Five campgrounds and several day-use facilities are located along Vt. 232 between US 2, north of Marshfield, and US 302, west of Groton.

The developed facilities and many of the area's bodies of water, mountains, and other points of interest are linked by an extensive network of hiking and multi-use trails, most of which are shown on the free hiking and snowmobile trail maps issued by FPR and available at the contact stations. The trails and major landmarks are also shown on a large map located in the Kettle Pond parking area. A pamphlet briefly describing the area's history and other publications concerning Groton State Forest may be obtained in season at the Nature Center, located just beyond the Big Deer camping area.

Heavy logging operations have been occurring and continue to occur in all parts of the Forest. These activities may disrupt portions of the trail system, so hikers should get current trail condition information from forest personnel. In some cases, trees have been marked for cutting with blue paint. Hikers should be careful to follow guide book trail descriptions in these areas.

Primitive camping is allowed in the forest, but there are certain restrictions. Check with forest personnel before camping away from the established campgrounds.

Peacham Pond Trail (1)

Marked with blue blazes and green diamonds, the trail begins in the New Discovery camping area, about ¾ m. below the contact station. Leaving the main camp road at a fork to the left (0.0 m.), the trail follows a well used woods road. Soon after beginning an easy descent, the trail reaches a junction on the right (0.3 m.) with the **New Discovery-Big Deer Trail (2)**. For the next 0.5 m. the trail passes through a logged area with several logging roads branching both left and right. Descending past an old road to the left (0.5 m.), which leads north 0.7 m. to Vt. 232, the trail continues straight ahead on easier grades to the end of the road. At this point another road comes in on the left.

Continuing straight ahead on easy up and down grades, the trail follows an older woods road which is not blazed but has occasional green diamonds and snowmobile signs. The trail reaches a fork (1.6 m.) where a spur on the left descends to a private camp on the south shore of **Peacham Pond**. Taking the right fork, the Peacham Pond Trail ascends for a short distance and then follows easy grades along a grassy woods road which is marked with occasional green or orange diamonds and snowmobile trail signs.

Eventually swinging to the north, the trail descends to cross **Sucker Brook** on a bridge **(2.1 m.)**. After continuing through an open wet area for some distance, the trail climbs through the woods to reaches a logging road (2.4 m.). To the right this road leads to Peacham village. Turning left on this road, the trail soon reaches its terminus at a road on the west shore of **Peacham Pond (2.6 m.)**. The road leads north and west for about 2¼ m. to Vt. 232.

New Discovery-Big Deer Trail (2)

Marked with blue blazes, the trail leaves the **Peacham Pond Trail (1)** 0.3 m. from the New Discovery campground road. From the junction (0.0 m.), the trail descends gradually through softwoods, crosses a stone wall (0.1 m.) and crosses the ends of two new logging roads. After leveling off, the trail follows the left side of a logged area and reaches a leanto (0.7 m.). After passing to the left of the leanto, the trail climbs gradually to a junction on the right (1.1 m.) with the **Osmore Pond-Big Deer Trail (5)**. The trail climbs steadily to the summit of **Big Deer Mt. (1.3 m.)**. From the 1992 ft. summit there is a view of Peacham Pond. Continuing along the ridge, the trail ends at an open rock area (1.4 m.) where there are good views of Lake Groton and other local landmarks.

New Discovery-Osmore Pond Trail (3)

Marked with blue blazes, the trail leaves the New Discovery campground road between the rest room facilities and the open camping field. From the road (0.0 m.), the trail descends through a spruce-fir stand and an old fuel wood logging area. It terminates at the **Osmore Pond Hiking Loop (4)** at the north end of **Osmore Pond (0.5 m.)**.

Osmore Pond Hiking Loop (4)

The blue-blazed trail begins at the Osmore Pond picnic shelter. From the shelter (0.0 m.), the trail descends to the shore and continues southerly through the picnic area. After following the shore for some distance and passing views across the pond of Big Deer Mt., the trail eventually bears away from the pond and reaches a junction (0.6 m.) with the **Little Deer Trail (6)** in a power line clearing. Returning to the woods, the trail soon crosses the outlet of Osmore Pond (0.7 m.) and then continues to a junction (0.8 m.) with the **Osmore Pond-Big Deer Trail (5)** and the **Hosmer Brook Trail (8).**

Turning to the left, the trail passes through an open area for some distance before entering deep woods and passing a leanto (1.2 m.). After passing another shelter (1.6 m.), the trail follows the shore back to the picnic shelter (2.0 m.).

Osmore Pond-Big Deer Trail (5)

Marked with blue blazes and a few orange diamonds, the trail leaves the **Osmore Pond Hiking Loop (4)** at its junction with the **Hosmer Brook Trail (8)** at the south end of the pond. From the junction (0.0 m.), the trail climbs over a low ridge (0.2 m.), crosses a wet sag on puncheon, and soon reaches a junction on the right (0.4 m.) with the **Coldwater Brook Trail (9).** The trail then ascends to a junction (0.7 m.) with the **New Discovery-Big Deer Trail (2).** To the right, it is 0.2 m. via the latter trail to the summit.

Little Deer Trail (6)

The blue-blazed trail leaves the **Osmore Pond Hiking Loop (4)** in a power line clearing, 0.6 m. south of the picnic shelter. From the junction (0.0 m.), the trail follows the line for a short distance before bearing to the right and climbing easily through the woods. At a sharp left turn (0.2 m.), the trail begins a steady climb to the wooded summit (elev. 1760 ft.) of **Little Deer Mt. (0.4 m.)** and then continues a short distance further to an open rock area (0.5 m.), where there is a good view of Lake Groton. Another open area to the right offers a good view of Spruce Mt.

New Discovery-Owl's Head Trail (7)

This blue blazed trail begins just below the maintenance area on the old road to Osmore Pond picnic shelter. From the road (0.0 m.), the trail enters the woods, passes through a timber stand improvement area, and continues with minor changes in elevation to cross a power line (0.2 m.). The trail soon begins to climb gradually and then more steeply to a low ridge (1.1 m.), then continues on easier grades to the upper end of the gravel road to the Owl's Head picnic area (1.5 m.).

Skirting the upper end of the parking loop, the trail passes to the left of the picnic shelter (1.7 m.) and climbs to the open summit (elev. 1958 ft.) of **Owl's Head Mt. (1.8 m.).** From the summit there are good views of Lake Groton, Kettle Pond, the White Mountains, and Green Mountains.

Hosmer Brook Trail (8)

Marked with blue blazes, the trail begins on the Boulder Beach access road, 1.3 m. from Vt. 232 and 0.3 m. beyond the entrance to the Stillwater camping area.

From the road (0.0 m.), the trail ascends gradually to the north on a woods road. Eventually reaching **Hosmer Brook (0.5 m.),** the trail follows the brook upstream to a junction (1.3 m.) with the **Osmore Pond Hiking Loop (4)** and the **Osmore Pond-Big Deer Trail (5).**

Coldwater Brook Trail (9)

The blue-blazed trail begins on the Boulder Beach access road, 1.8 m. from Vt. 232 and 0.3 m. beyond the entrance to the Big Deer camping area. From the road (0.0 m.) the trail scrambles up the bank on the left side of the brook and continues with little change in elevation to a crossing (0.4 m.) of the **Peacham Bog Trail (10).** Continuing along or near **Coldwater Brook,** the trail slabs around a low knoll, passes two large boulders on the left (0.6 m.) and crosses a logged area. The trail stays close to the brook and crosses two small streams (0.7 m.). Soon after crossing two larger streams, the trail reaches the stonework of an old sawmill (1.1 m.), one of several which at one time used the waters of Coldwater Brook.

From the sawmill site, the trail ascends to a junction (1.2 m.), turns left, and ascends on easy grades over occasional rough footing. After passing through an area marked for logging the trail reaches a junction (2.0 m.) with the **Osmore Pond-Big Deer Trail (5)**, 0.4 m. above the latter's junction with the **Hosmer Brook Trail (8)**.

Peacham Bog Trail (10)

Note: Part of this **trail** has been **temporarily blocked** by logging operations. Hikers should check with forest personnel regarding the current status of this route. The **Martin's Pond Trail (11)** provides an alternate route to Peacham Bog from the east.

Marked with blue blazes and orange diamonds, the trail begins at the northeast corner of the Nature Center parking area. From the parking area (0.0 m.), the trail climbs an embankment and then descends gradually through the woods to a crossing of the **Coldwater Brook Trail (9)**. A short distance beyond, the trail crosses the brook on a bridge (0.4 m.). The trail follows the brook downstream for a short distance and then resumes an easterly direction as it begins an easy ascent along old woods roads. After crossing a small stream (1.5 m.) and cresting a low ridge (1.5 m.), the trail descends on easy grades into a shallow sag (2.4 m.) and then continues past a view to the north of Devil's Hill to an overgrown clearing and a junction on the right (2.6 m.) with the **Martin's Pond Trail (11)**.

At the junction, the Peacham Bog Trail turns sharply to the left and follows a logging road. Turning left at the next junction (2.8 m.), the trail follows badly overgrown and poorly marked routing for several hundred feet before descending gradually on an old road and entering **Peacham Bog (3.0 m.)**. The trail penetrates the bog for a short distance before ending at a sign (3.1 m.). Because of the fragile nature of the bog environment, to say nothing of the possibility of losing one's way, the hiker should remain on the trail.

Martin's Pond Trail (11)

This trail leaves the **Peacham Bog Trail (10)** in a clearing 2.6 m. from the Nature Center. For the most part a primitive road, the trail crosses Red Brook and follows the road to its terminus (1.6 m.). Here a public road leads north for about 1.5 m. to **Martin's Pond.**

Kettle Pond Hiking Loop (12)

Marked with blue blazes, the trail begins at the Kettle Pond parking area on Vt. 232. From the parking area (0.0 m.) the trail leads to a junction (0.2 m.) a short distance before reaching the pond. The left fork follows the south shore of the pond. Turning right, the trail passes a leanto on a short spur to the right and continues through the woods to a left turn (0.5 m.). The trail passes through a wet area and continues along or near the shore. After passing through an area of large boulders at the site of an old camp (0.8 m.), the trail continues past the site of a leanto (1.2 m.). The trail bears right and shortly passes another leanto (1.7 m.). Circling the end of **Kettle Pond,** the trail traverses some wet and rocky areas. After passing a private camp, the trail climbs over and around some large boulders and reaches a new shelter. The trail remains in the vicinity of the shoreline and reaches the **Kettle Pond Group Camping Area (3.0 m.).** After crossing **Stillwater Brook** on some driftwood logs the trail completes the loop at a junction (3.1 m.). Bearing right, the trail returns to the parking area (3.3 m.).

Abandoned Railroad Grade (13)

Completed in 1873, the Montpelier and Wells River Railroad, known in its final years as the Barre and Chelsea Railroad, for many years did a prosperous business hauling granite, milk, lumber, and "summer people" between Montpelier and a Boston and Maine connection at Woodsville. Following a long decline in business, the railroad was abandoned in 1957. In addition to a major station in the now nearly deserted community of Lanesboro, there were flag stops at Lakeside and Rocky Pond serving campers on Lake Groton.

Within Groton State Forest, the roadbed remains well defined for about 7 m. between the old Edgewater station on Marshfield Pond and Ricker Mills. Beyond Ricker Mills, the roadbed continues on private property to US 302, west of Groton.

Silver Ledge Trail (14)

Marked with blue blazes, the trail begins at a logging road 0.7 m. west of Vt. 232. The logging road leaves the highway 1.0 m. north of the Ricker Pond camping area and 3.5 m. south of the Kettle Pond parking area.

From the logging road (0.0 m.), the **Silver Ledge Trail** bears right into the woods, quickly crosses Beaver Brook and then begins a winding climb. After passing a view of Lake Groton (0.5 m.), the trail continues past several other views and eventually reaches the 1838 ft. summit of **Silver Ledge** at a large boulder in the woods **(0.6 m.).**

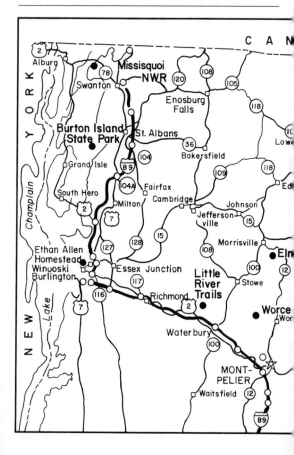

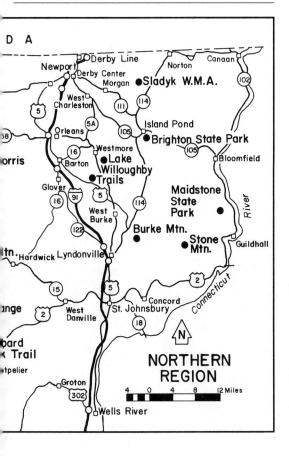

NORTHERN REGION

The northern region contains all of Grand Isle, Franklin, Orleans, and Lamoille Counties. Parts of Chittenden, Washington, Caledonia, and Essex Counties are also within the region.

Lake Champlain, with its scenic islands and peninsulas, attains its greatest width in this region. Fossil remains and the traces of old shorelines are reminders of times when the lake was much larger, and also when it was an arm of the ocean.

The Green Mountains dominate the central part of the region, and attain their greatest height at the Chin of Mt. Mansfield (elevation 4393 ft.), the highest point in Vermont. The Main Range continues north into Canada, and is known there as the Sutton Mountains. Further east, the Third Range is known as the Worcester Mountains north of the Winooski River, and as the Lowell Mountains north of the Lamoille River.

East of the Green Mountains is the narrow, northern end of the Vermont Piedmont. The area is noted for its many lakes and ponds, with Lake Memphremagog and Lake Willoughby being the best known.

The northeastern corner of Vermont is commonly known as the Northeast Kingdom, and is sparsely populated and heavily wooded. Geologists call this physiographic region the Northeastern Highlands. It mostly consists of more than 125 randomly scattered mountains and high hills. Heavy glaciation has resulted in several large lakes and ponds, among them Maidstone Lake and Averill Lake. However, poor drainage is responsible for extensive areas of swamp and muskeg, adding further to the difficulties of foot travel and route finding.

Ethan Allen Homestead

This area, which is managed by the Winooski Valley Park District, is located in the north end of Burlington. There are two trails located on the property. The **Wetlands Trail** is a self-guided nature trail that is about ¼ mile in length. There is also a 2 mile walk around the periphery of the lower meadow that follows the edge of the **Winooski River** and passes a sandy beach.

To reach the Homestead, take the "North Ave. Beaches" exit off Vt. 127 (Beltline Northern Connector) in North Burlington and follow the small green highway signs. The driveway to the Homestead begins off the highway's exit ramp to North Avenue. Once in the park, the nature trail begins on the right, off of the dirt road leading to the picnic shelter. An interpretive brochure is available from the information box at the main parking area near the barn.

Burton Island State Park

Located on an island in St. Albans Bay (see USGS St. Albans Bay), Burton Island State Park (camping only) is accessible only by boat. A nature trail and two hiking trails are located on the island. A park naturalist is on duty during the camping season.

From US 7 in St. Albans, follow Vt. 36 west about 4 m. to St. Albans Bay. Then continue on Town Rd., Lake Rd., and Point Rd. southwest for about 3½ m. to the Kill Kare area, where vehicles may be parked and boats launched.

Missisquoi National Wildlife Refuge

This 5,600 acre area, managed by the U.S. Fish and Wildlife Service, was established to provide feeding and resting habitat for migratory waterfowl. The refuge occupies much of the Missisquoi River delta and consists of marsh, open water, and wooded swamp. There is a 1½ mile interpretive trail, located behind the headquarters building, that is open from daylight to dark throughout the year. In addition, there are other areas suitable for observing birds and other wildlife.

The refuge is located near the eastern shore of Lake Champlain. The headquarters building is approximately 2 m. west of Swanton, on the south side of Vt. 78.

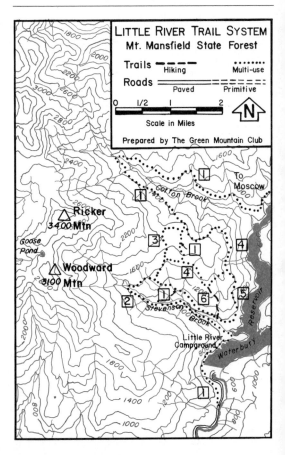

LITTLE RIVER TRAIL SYSTEM
Mt. Mansfield State Forest

Trails ▬ ▬ ▬   ••••••••
        Hiking   Multi-use

Roads ═══════   ════════
          Paved   Primitive

0   1/2   1   2

Scale in Miles

Prepared by The Green Mountain Club

LITTLE RIVER AREA

The Little River block of the Mt. Mansfield State Forest comprises several thousand acres surrounding the Waterbury Reservoir and extending westerly to the Green Mountain ridgeline (see USGS Bolton Mountain). The Little River Campground (no day use facilities) is located on the southwest shore of the reservoir and is reached by following a road north 3½ m. from US 2, about 1½ m. west of Waterbury.

Below the dam, to the west of the access road, there are extensive clearings, where a large Civilian Conservation Corps (CCC) camp was located during construction of the Dam (1934-38). Only the old roads and a few chimneys and foundations remain of the self-contained community of more than 80 buildings in which more than 2000 men once lived and worked.

The Stevenson Brook—Ricker Basin area, north and west of the campground, was once well populated by several dozen families which depended on subsistence farming and small water-powered mills for a precarious living. Depletion of the thin soil, the harsh environment, and better economic opportunities elsewhere led to gradual depopulation of the area, beginning about one hundred years ago and ending about 1930, when the land was acquired for the flood control dam. Much of the land has since been reclaimed by the forest or covered by water, but numerous reminders of the past remain in the form of stone walls, cellar holes, cemeteries, and old clearings where lilacs and apple trees still grow. A number of the Ricker Basin sites are identified and briefly described in a history hike brochure and trail map available without charge at the Little River Campground.

The Little River trails generally follow old town roads and woods roads. Most are maintained as multi-use trails and are marked with orange diamonds, supplemented at times with blue blazes.

The Waterbury parking area, located 1.7 m. north of US 2, provides convenient access to the beginning of the Little River Trail. For more convenient access to Ricker Basin, make parking arrangements with the Little River Campground manager.

The number assigned to each trail in the text is used to identify that trail on the system map.

Little River Trail (1)

This main route in the Little River trail system follows circuitous routing for more than 12 miles between the Waterbury and Moscow parking lots, connecting en route with the other area trails. A multi-purpose trail, its orange diamond markers are supplemented with blue paint blazes in some sections. Portions of the trail follow paved or gravel roads.

From the Waterbury parking area (0.0 m.), the Little River Trail immediately enters an overgrown clearing and turns to the right. Soon leaving the clearing, the trail follows a woods road uphill to a power line crossing in a large clearing and an unmarked junction on the right with the **North CCC Loop (0.1 m.).**

Rejoining the main trail in about ¼ m., the **North CCC Loop** follows the power line northerly through extensive clearings where a stone chimney, old foundations, and other obscure remains of a CCC camp (1934-38) can be seen. More evidence of CCC days can be observed in other clearings to the north.

From the power line, the Little River Trail continues a short distance westerly to a much smaller clearing, where it turns right (0.2 m.). The trail follows a grassy road north through several small clearings, meeting the north end of the **North CCC Loop** at the power line (0.4 m.) and then joining a woods road from the left (0.5 m.), which it follows to the Little River Road (0.6 m.). To the right, it is 0.6 m. south via the road to the Waterbury parking area.

The trail follows the paved Little River Road uphill, passes the Waterbury Dam (1.0 m.), and reaches the end of the pavement at the entrance to the Little River Campground (1.7 m.). After continuing along the road with little change in elevation, the trail bears left off the campground road at the lower end of the **Stevenson Brook Trail (2) (1.9 m.).** The Little River Trail then descends easily along an old road to **Stevenson Brook (2.4 m.).** Here the trail turns to the right, fords the brook, and follows an old road uphill to a small clearing, where the **Dolley Road Trail (5)** leaves to the right **(2.6 m.).** The Little River Trail turns left at the junction and ascends northwesterly along one of the original town roads, soon passing the site of the Bert Goodell farm (Marker #3). After crossing a small brook on a plank bridge (3.1 m.), the trail reaches Marker #4 at the Almeron Goodell place

(3.3 m.). Of the several dozen buildings once located in the Little River—Ricker Basin area, this abandoned homestead, dubbed Camp Comfort by winter travelers, is the only one remaining.

Continuing along the road, the trail ascends through several clearings and crosses several small streams. After passing through the Patsy Herbert farm site (Marker #5), from which there is a view of the Worcester Range, the trail reaches an old road junction, where the upper end of the **Stevenson Brook Trail** leaves to the left **(3.7 m.).** From the junction, the Little River Trail ascends easily in a northerly direction along the stone walls and overgrown clearing of the former Curt Montgomery farm (Marker #8) to the south end of the **Patterson Trail (3)** at a road junction known as **Ricker Corners (4.1 m.).** To the left on a wooded slope is a small cemetery with a dozen or more headstones, about half of which are still legible.

At Ricker Corners the Little River Trail takes the right fork and ascends easily to the east along the old town road, passing the Carney farm site (Marker #10) and the Ricker School site (Marker #11) on the left before reaching the south end of the **Ricker Lot Trail (4) (4.4 m.).** The Little River Trail turns sharply to the left at the junction and soon begins an increasingly steep climb to the north. After crossing a spur ridge (4.7 m.), the trail descends gradually through several small clearings, where there are limited views to the east, to a junction on the left with the north end of the **Patterson Trail (5.0 m.).** The trail then returns to the woods and descends easily to a junction with the north end of the Ricker Lot Trail at **Kelty Corners (5.1 m.),** near which the two Kelty farms were located.

From Kelty Corners, the Little River Trail bears to the left onto a recently used woods road and descends, steadily at first and then more gradually, toward the northwest. After crossing a small brook on a plank bridge (5.5 m.) and passing remnants of stone walls near the wooded site of an old farm (5.8 m.), the trail ascends very gradually and offers occasional views of Bolton Mt. and neighboring Green Mountain peaks. Eventually reaching a more permanent section of the road, the trail crosses the **left fork** of **Cotton Brook** on a wooden bridge **(6.8 m.)** and assumes a more northerly course through open areas which provide views of Ricker Mt., Bolton Mt., and Mt. Dewey. A short distance upstream from the remains of an up and down sawmill, the trail crosses the **main branch** of **Cotton Brook** on a large steel culvert **(7.2 m.).**

Ascending from the stream crossing, the Little River Trail swings sharply to the east, immediately crosses a tributary brook on a plank bridge, and begins a long descent on easy to moderate grades past several old clearings and apple orchards marking the sites of abandoned farms. Some distance after coming within sight of **Cotton Brook,** the trail begins a gradual swing to the north (9.7 m.) and eventually reaches a closed gate at the state forest boundary (11.6 m.). The trail then follows the public Cotton Brook Road to a parking lot, where the trail ends (12.4 m.). From the parking lot, it is 0.2 m. to the Nebraska Notch Road, from which point it is about 1.5 m. to Moscow village and 2.1 m. to Vt. 100.

Stevenson Brook Trail (2)

Marked with orange diamonds and blue blazes, the trail begins where the Little River Trail leaves the campground road, 0.2 m. from the campground entrance.

Leaving the **Little River Trail (1) (0.0 m.),** the Stevenson Brook Trail follows an old road upstream on easy grades. After crossing the brook twice on bridges (0.5 and 0.6 m.), the trail reaches a clearing (0.9 m.). A spur to the right leads to the ruins of the Waterbury Last Block Company's steam powered sawmill, which operated until 1922. Among the ruins are one of the boilers and parts of the large band saws.

The trail continues through the clearing on an old road, crosses a small stream on a plank bridge (1.0 m.), and bears to the left at a fork (1.1 m.). After a short steep climb, the trail descends to cross **Stevenson Brook** on a wooden bridge **(1.3 m.).** The trail then turns sharply to the right and follows the road uphill. After passing between old stone walls and crossing the second of two small streams (1.4 m.), the trail begins an easy descent and crosses another small brook (1.7 m.). Shortly, the trail ends at a junction with the **Little River Trail (1.8 m.).** To the right, it is 1.8 m. via the Little River Trail back to the Stevenson Brook Trail's beginning.

Patterson Trail (3)

Marked with orange diamonds, the Patterson Trail leaves the **Little River Trail (1)** at **Ricker Corners (0.0 m.)** and ascends the left fork of the road. The trail reaches the end of the road in a large clearing marking the site of the former Alexander Patterson farm (0.1 m.). The trail then turns to the left, follows somewhat obscure routing uphill through the overgrown field, and returns to the woods (0.2 m.). After crossing a low ridge (0.5 m.) and descending along its west flank for some distance, the trail turns to the right at an old woods road junction (0.7 m.) and descends gradually to the east to rejoin the **Little River Trail** in a bushy clearing **(0.8 m.)**. From this point it is 0.9 m. back to Ricker Corners via the Little River Trail.

Ricker Lot Trail (4)

Marked with orange diamonds and occasional blue blazes, the trail leaves the **Little River Trail (1)** 0.3 m. east of Ricker Corners.

From the junction (0.0 m.), the Ricker Lot Trail trends easterly, following an old town road on easy grades beside stone walls and quickly passing the site of the William Clossey farm (Marker #12). Soon after starting a gradual descent, the trail detours to the left (0.2 m.) and descends through an old field to skirt a beaver dam which covers the site of the barn on the former Andrew Burley farm (Marker #13). Quickly returning to the road, the trail continues downhill past a clearing marking the site of the Tom Herbert farm (Marker #14) (0.5 m.) to a junction with the **Hedgehog Hill Trail (6) (0.7 m.)**.

From the junction, the Ricker Lot Trail turns to the left and skirts the upper edge of an old field, following an old farm road. Bearing to the right at a fork (0.8 m.), the trail descends steadily for some distance. After crossing a small stream in a small clearing (0.9 m.), the trail climbs gradually to a junction on the right with the upper end of the **Dolley Road Trail (5) (1.1 m.)**.

From the junction, the Ricker Lot Trail assumes a northerly direction and climbs very gradually through the woods. After crossing a stone wall (1.3 m.), the trail follows easy up and down grades along the shoulder of the ridge. Eventually swinging more to the northwest (1.8 m.), the trail begins a steady descent. After making a pronounced swing to the south, the trail climbs steadily for some distance before assuming a northwesterly direction on easier grades. After passing a stone wall (3.0 m.) and crossing an old road in a small clearing (3.1 m.), the trail descends gradually to **Kelty Corners** and a junction with the **Little River Trail (3.2 m.).**

Dolley Road Trail (5)

Although misspelled or corrupted, the old road and trail are named after the Dan Dalley family, which once farmed at the lower end of the road near the present campground road. Marked with orange diamonds and blue blazes, the trail leaves the Little River Trail 0.1 m. above the Stevenson Brook crossing and 0.9 m. from the campground entrance.

From its junction with the **Little River Trail (1) (0.0 m.),** the Dolley Road Trail trends easterly on easy grades, crosses a stream on a plank bridge (0.3 m.), and descends to a junction on the left with the **Hedgehog Hill Trail (6) (0.4 m.).** The trail then continues its easy descent to a junction with the campground road (0.6 m.). To the right, the road leads south 0.6 m. to the campground entrance.

Turning to the left, the Dolley Road Trail follows the campground road to campsite #59 (0.8 m.), where it turns to the left and begins an increasingly steep climb on the old Dolley Road. After passing a large boulder on the right (1.3 m.), the trail bears to the left at an old fork (1.5 m.) and ascends on easier grades through old clearings past the foundations and apple trees of the former Ezra Fuller farm (1.6 m.). The trail then crosses a stone wall (1.7 m.) and continues to a junction with the **Ricker Lot Trail (4) (1.8 m.).** To the left, it is 0.4 m. to the upper end of the Hedgehog Hill Trail and 1.4 m. to the Little River Trail at Ricker Corners.

Hedgehog Hill Trail (6)

The trail begins on the **Dolley Road Trail (5),** 0.2 m. west of its southern junction with the campground road and 0.4 m. east of the Little River Trail (1).

From the junction (0.0 m.), the trail climbs steadily to the northwest on an old town road, soon crossing a brook on a bridge (0.1 m.) and reaching a fork (0.2 m.). The trail takes the less steep right branch, but the two branches eventually rejoin (0.4 m.). After passing between stone walls, the trail reaches an old clearing and foundations of the former Gideon Ricker Farm (Marker #17) (0.5 m.). Continuing uphill along the road, the trail soon comes to the private Ricker family cemetery (Marker #16) on the left (0.6 m.). A short distance beyond, the trail reaches a junction with the **Ricker Lot Trail (4) (0.7 m.).** To the right, the Ricker Lot Trail leads 0.4 m. to the upper end of the Dolley Road Trail. Straight ahead, it is 1.0 m. to Ricker Corners.

Hubbard Park

Located in the City of Montpelier, 121-acre Hubbard Park offers a variety of recreational opportunities including picnic areas, a softball field, trails for hiking and skiing, and a fifty-foot observation tower with spectacular views of the surrounding mountain ranges.

A map of the Hubbard Park Trails is published by the Montpelier Park Commission, and a self-guiding Nature Trail booklet is available at the beginning of the trail.

From the intersection of Main and State Streets in downtown Montpelier, head north on Vermont Route 12. In half a mile turn left onto Winter St. and proceed uphill a short distance to the Park Entrance.

TRAIL EROSION CONTROL

Erosion control on hiking trails takes many forms. Waterbars, made of log or stone, are placed across the trail at an angle to direct running water off the trail. Steps, also made of log or stone, are used to stabilize the trail on steep slopes and to keep soil from being carried downslope. Cribbing is used to hold the treadway in place where the trail crosses a steep side slope. Hikers can assist in erosion control by staying on the trail instead of walking around these structures.

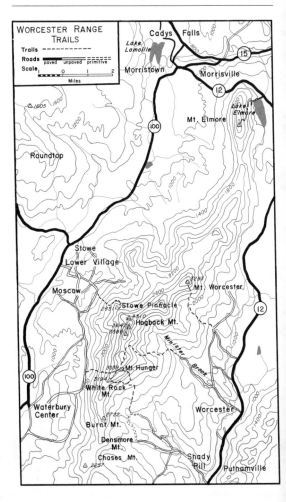

WORCESTER RANGE
TRAILS

Trails --------
Roads ====== paved unpaved primitive
Scale   0   1   2
         Miles

WORCESTER MOUNTAINS

Between the Winooski and Lamoille rivers, the Third Range of the Green Mountain is known as the Worcester Mountains (see USGS Montpelier, Middlesex, Stowe, Mount Worcester, Hyde Park). Of the dozen or so prominent peaks in the range, Mt. Hunger (3586 ft.) is the most conspicuous and best known. However, the highest point (3642 ft.) is an officially nameless peak sometimes referred to as Mt. Putnam, located about 2 m. north of Mt. Hunger.

From White Rock Mt. north, much of the range is included in Putnam State Forest. The northernmost peak, Elmore Mountain, is in Elmore State Park. The Vermont Dept. of Forests, Parks, and Recreation is working on major changes and additions to the Worcester Range hiking trails. State crews will make every effort to keep the trails clearly marked, but hikers should be aware that changes in the existing system can occur at any time.

Elmore Mountain Trail

Although one of the lowest peaks in the Worcester Mountains, Elmore Mt. (USGS Hyde Park) probably offers the most varied and interesting views, due to its isolated location at the north end of the range and its commanding view of the pastoral Lamoille River valley. There is an old fire tower on the summit, but it is in disrepair. The trail to the summit begins in Elmore State Park (campground, picnic area, swimming). The park entrance is located on the west side of Vt. 12, a short distance north of the village of Lake Elmore. Pay the small day use fee and make parking arrangements at the park contact station.

Continuing straight ahead from the contact station, the road passes the camping area and begins to ascend on an old CCC road (0.0 m.). The road reaches a chained gate near a picnic shelter (0.5 m.). From this point on the trail is blue-blazed.

The trail continues on the road through the gate and ascends to the south. Near the end of the road, the trail turns sharply to the right (1.0 m.) at a blue arrow and sign on a tree and follows a well worn path through open woods. After some steady climbing in places, the trail reaches a grassy clearing a short distance below the ridge (1.9 m.). The cellar hole on the left marks where the old lookout's cabin once stood. Here, overlooking Lake Elmore, there is a good view to the east.

To the right, on the west side of the clearing, the trail begins a steep and winding climb over rocks. Soon it reaches a level area and a trail junction. To the right is the **Balanced Rock Trail.** To the left the Elmore Mountain Trail continues about 100 ft. to the old fire tower on the summit (2.1 m.).

From the tower or, to a lesser extent, from the open rocks to the south, there are impressive views of the Green Mountains from the Jay Peak area south to the Lincoln Range, the Worcester Range, the Lamoille valley, the Waterbury Reservoir, Burke Mt., and various peaks in the Northeast Kingdom.

SUMMARY: Picnic area to summit, 2.1 m.; 1450 ft. ascent; 1¾ hr. (Rev. 1 hr.).

Balanced Rock Trail

This blue-blazed trail begins at the junction with the **Elmore Mt. Trail** north of the Elmore Mt. fire tower. From the junction (0.0 m.), the trail follows easy grades just east of ridgeline to a cleared view to the east (0.1 m.). Continuing in the woods for some distance, the trail then crosses to the west side of the ridge (0.3 m.) and soon reaches an open rock area (0.4 m.), where there is an excellent view of the Stowe valley and the Mt. Mansfield area. Quickly returning to the east side of the ridge, the trail descends through the woods to another vantage point overlooking Lake Elmore and then continues a short distance further to the cigar-shaped **Balanced Rock (0.5 m.).**

Moss Glen Falls

Recently acquired by the State of Vermont, this attractive falls is located in the northeast corner of Stowe. It should not be confused with the more spectacular falls of the same name in Granville Gulf.

From Vt. 100, 3.1 m. north of the intersection of Vt. 100 and Vt. 108 in Stowe village, turn right onto Randolph Rd. (0.0 m.). Turn right at the next fork (0.4 m.) onto Moss Glen Falls Rd. and continue to another fork (0.9 m.). The paved road turns right and crosses a bridge. The trail to the falls follows the old road that continues straight ahead. There is limited parking at the junction.

Following the old road, swampy in places, into the field

ahead of the parking area, the trail soon angles off the road to the right into the woods in the direction of the sound of the falls. Soon a short, steep ascent reaches a lookout down into the bowl of the falls (0.4 m.).

Worcester Mountain Trail

Located in the northwest corner of the town of Worcester, the summit (USGS Mount Worcester) offers good views of the Green Mountains, the Lamoille valley, and the northern White Mountains.

The trailhead is reached from the village of Worcester, on Vt. 12 north of Montpelier. Take the first left (Minister Brook Rd.) off the highway a short distance north of the Worcester Town Hall (0.0 m.), and follow this road west to Hampshire Hill Rd. (1.5 m.).

Turn right on Hampshire Hill Rd. and ascend steadily. After passing a road which doubles back to the right (3.8 m.), turn left into a narrow lane just after crossing a brook below a small, red, remodeled schoolhouse (3.9 m.). Continue up the lane and bear right by a mobile home on the left (4.0 m.). Continue past a road to the right to a clearing with ample parking (4.1 m.).

From the clearing (0.0 m.), the trail follows the same gravel woods road northwest into the woods where the blue-blazes begin and the gravel road turns into a dirt woods road. The road crosses a ditch, crosses two small streams, and eventually parallels **Hancock Brook** off to the left; it soon reaches a level, grassy area where a road branches off to the right. The trail continues straight ahead a short distance on the road and into the trees where the dirt road narrows into a level trail (0.8 m.).

Soon bearing away from the brook, the trail continues in a birch tree hollow where it crosses two smaller streams (1.1 m. and 1.5 m.) and then climbs steadily north and NW to an attractive ledge crossing of another small stream (1.6 m.).

The trail then continues its steady climb into a shallow sag (2.2 m.) where almost at the top it turns sharply back to the left, although a dead-end path continues straight ahead. Now, following blue-blazes mostly on rocks, the trail begins a rough ascent over rocks and through thick scrub to the open summit of **Mt. Worcester (2.5 m.).**

SUMMARY: Road to summit, 2.5 m.; 1970 ft. ascent; 2¼ hr. (Rev. 1¼ hr.).

Stowe Pinnacle Trail

From this prominent spur (elev. 2651 ft.) on the northwest side of Hogback Mountain (USFS Stowe), there are excellent views Mt. Mansfield and other peaks in the Green Mountains. The trail has recently been relocated onto state land.

From Vt. 100, about 1½ m. south of the village of Stowe, turn east on Gold Brook Rd. opposite the Nichols Farm Lodge (0.0 m.). Bear left at the first fork (0.3 m.) and follow Gold Brook upstream through an intersection at the covered bridge (1.2 m.), then turn right at the next junction (1.8 m.). Continue to the trailhead and parking area on the left (2.3 m.).

From the parking area (0.0 m.) the trail passes from abandoned pasture to a mixed forest and crosses a stream (0.5 m.). The trail now begins a steeper climb by a series of wide switchbacks through mature woods to a notch just below Stowe Pinnacle (0.9 m.). The trail makes a steep climb from the notch to a ledge on the left (1.0 m.), then continues along the contour to a junction with the former route (1.2 m.). Continuing on easy grades through scrub growth, the trail soon reaches the open summit (1.4 m.).

SUMMARY: Parking lot to summit, 1.4 m.; 1520 ft. ascent; 1½ hr. (Rev. 1 hr.).

Mount Hunger

Although the north summit (3586 ft.) of this well-known mountain (USGS Stowe) is heavily wooded, the bald south summit (3539 ft.) is famous for its blueberries and its excellent views of the Green Mountains and the White Mountains. There are direct routes to the south summit from the east and west, a longer route from the north, and an indirect route from the south via White Rock Mt.

Worcester Trail

This blue-blazed route is the longest of the Mt. Hunger trails.

From the village of Worcester on Vt. 12 (0.0 m.), follow Minister Brook Rd. past Hampshire Hill Rd. (1.5 m.) on the right, and continue to the end of the road at the Richardson farm (3.5 m.). Make parking arrangements at the farm, but be certain not to block driveways or roads if no one is home.

From the farm (0.0 m.), the trail passes between the barn on the right and a small building on the left, following an old road on the left of the field and soon crossing an electric fence (0.3 m.) across the road. The trail then continues on the road to a clearing, ignores a fork to the right (0.7 m.) in the clearing and crosses a brook (0.8 m.). The trail then follows what is now a woods road, keeping straight ahead and ignoring any forks to the left or right. The trail nears a small brook on the left (2.0 m.), turns left and crosses the brook.

Continuing on a gradual switch-back path, the trail climbs steadily through the woods and soon crosses a brook just above an attractive waterfall (2.4 m.). The trail then begins a steep climb past an undeveloped lookout to the east (2.8 m.) and continues to the base of a steep ledge (3.1 m.). Skirting the ledges, the trail then makes a steep and winding climb over the ridge to a view to the west (3.2 m.). Turning to the south and remaining below the ridge, the trail descends for some distance and then climbs steadily to a point near the north summit (3.9 m.). Here the beginning of the Skyline Trail system departs to the right. This system, which is still under construction, will eventually connect the major peaks of the Worcester Range.

Eventually leaving deep woods and passing through intermittent scrub, the trail passes over several rocky knobs and then ascends to the south summit of **Mt. Hunger (4.4 m.)**.

SUMMARY: Richardson farm to south summit, 4.4 m.; 1950 ft. ascent; 3¼ hr. (Rev. 2¼ hr.).

Middlesex Trail

Most of this blue-blazed trail follows the route of a carriage road built in 1877 by the proprietors of the Pavilion Hotel in Montpelier to transport guests up the mountain. A short trail, complete with wooden stairways to ease the steep climb over the ledges, connected the end of the road and the summit.

From Montpelier, follow Vt. 12 north past the Wrightsville Dam to a junction on the left with the Shady Rill Rd. (0.0 m.). Follow the road westerly up a long hill through the Hamlet of Shady Rill (1.2 m.) and continue to Worcester Road (the first road to the right) at a four corners (2.2 m.). Turn right onto Worcester Road (0.0 m.) and continue over a one-lane bridge. Pass a road on the right (0.5 m.) and turn left (0.7 m.) onto another road.

After passing a private drive on the left (1.6 m.), continue through the woods past a private drive to a large residence up to the right (2.2 m.) with a tall windmill in the front yard. The road continues to a large clearing and junction with a logging road to the right (2.5 m.) which is the road the trail starts on. Ample parking is available at the junction.

From the road junction (0.0 m.), the trail follows the logging road to the right through the fields and soon enters the woods where blue-blazes are seen. Ascending on easy grades, the trail eventually reaches a junction on the right (0.8 m.) with a recently discontinued alternate approach route.

The trail then climbs along the road to a marked junction on the left with the White Rock Trail (1.6 m.). Here the trail swings to the right and begins ascending an unmarked rock spur on the right (1.9 m.), which leads about 125 ft. to views to the east and south.

Climbing steadily at times, the trail skirts the base of ledges for some distance before coming to an apparent dead-end where it suddenly swings sharply up a ledge to the left (2.5 m.). It then climbs steeply in the open to the south summit, following blue-blazes on rocks and trees, and an unmarked junction with the Waterbury Trail and Worcester Trail (2.8 m.). Care should be taken to note where the trail comes out on the summit for blazing is sometimes obscure.

From the summit, nearly every peak in the Main Range of the Green Mountains is visible from Whiteface Mt. in the north to Killington Peak in the south. A number of Adirondack peaks are visible to the west beyond Lake Champlain. To the east, Mt. Washington and the Presidential Range, Mt. Moosilauke, and the Franconia Range can be seen in the distance, while Burke Mt. and Bald Mt. are among the numerous northeast Vermont mountains nearer at hand. Directly to the south are most of the other peaks in the Worcester Range.

SUMMARY: Road to summit, 2.8 m.; 1900 ft. ascent; 2½ hr. (Rev. 1½ hr.).

Waterbury Trail

This blue-blazed trail from the west begins on Water Works Rd., north of Waterbury Center.

From Waterbury Center village (0.0 m.), east of Vt. 100, follow Maple St. north. Take the first right onto Loomis Hill Rd. (0.2 m.) and follow it to a fork (2.7 m.). Take the left fork, Water Works Rd., and continue to a parking lot on the right near an abandoned stone quarry (3.7 m.).

From the parking area (0.0 m.), the trail begins a moderate climb through a mixed hardwood forest. After crossing a stream (0.9 m.), the trail leads up over several long sections of ledge and crosses an old, red-blazed state land boundary. The trail swings to the right, climbs steeply, and crosses a second stream (1.2 m.). Bearing left, the trail levels out before reaching a third stream crossing (1.5 m.).

Beyond the stream, the **White Rock Trail** branches to the right **(1.7 m.).** From the junction, the Waterbury Trail ascends straight ahead steeply on rocks in the open to a **junction** with the **Middlesex** and **Worcester Trails** on the **south summit (1.9 m.).**

SUMMARY: Water Works Road to summit, 1.9 m.; 2290 ft. ascent; 2 hr. (Rev. 1 hr.).

White Rock Trail

This blue-blazed trail provides access to the summit of White Rock Mt. (elev. 3194 ft.) from both the Middlesex and Waterbury Trails. It covers a wide variety of terrain in a short distance, and can be quite tricky and challenging.

Leaving the **Middlesex Trail** 1.6 m. from its trailhead **(0.0 m.),** the White Rock Trail ascends steeply through the woods to a junction (0.7 m.). To the left, a **spur** trail leads 0.2 m. south to the summit of **White Rock Mt.**

Taking the right fork at the junction, the White Rock Trail descends to a wet area (0.9 m.). The trail then climbs around numerous boulders at or near the ridge to its terminus at the **Waterbury Trail (1.5 m.).** To the right it is 0.2 m. to the summit of Mt. Hunger.

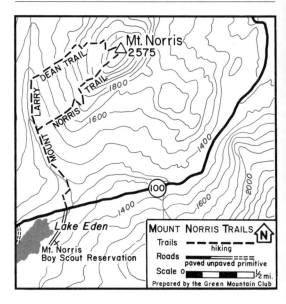

MOUNT NORRIS

Located in the town of Eden, the summit (elev. 2575 ft.) and several lower vantage points on this distinctively shaped peak (USGS Hardwick) offer good local views to the south and more distant views of the Worcester Range and the Green Mountains. Two blue-blazed trails with a common beginning on Vt. 100 are maintained by the campers and staff of the nearby Mount Norris Scout Reservation and form a continuous loop over the mountain.

The trails begin on the west side of Vt. 100, just north of the entrance to the Scout reservation, 2.0 m. north of Eden Mills and 6.1 m. south of Vt. 58 in Lowell village. The unmarked trailhead is at a gravel pit road which heads west through an old field. Ample parking is available beside the highway.

Mount Norris Trail

This is the older and steeper direct route to the summit. From Vt. 100 (0.0 m.), the trail follows the gravel pit road west for a short distance and then angles to the right onto an overgrown old road just before reaching a line of trees (0.1 m.). The trail follows the old road to the northwest corner of the field (0.2 m.) into the trees by a brook where the first blue (and sometimes orange or both orange and blue) blazes appear, and then follows the badly washed road upstream across a collapsed bridge (0.3 m.). The trail continues on the road near the brook on an easy upward winding grade, following the orange and blue tree markings, for some distance and then comes into the lower end of a large clearing, where there is an unmarked junction with the **Larry Dean Trail (0.7 m.).** Crossing to the upper edge of the clearing, the road divides and the Mount Norris Trail enters the woods to the right at a tall red painted iron pipe and ascends steadily for some distance on an old woods road following blue and orange markings. After a short distance, the road (a narrow path at times) turns right at a big rock on the ground. Continuing upward, the trail comes to and then swings to the right of a huge rock at the base of a rock ledge (1.1 m.) and begins a steep and winding climb around the ledge.

Resuming a northerly direction, the trail continues a steep, difficult upward climb through rocks to a partially open rock area, where there are good views to the south and east (1.3 m.). Pink ribbons tied on tree branches are used along with the blue and orange to mark the trail from here to the summit.

The trail, narrow and overgrown from here to the summit, passes several more limited views on and off the trail before ascending to what appears to be a wooded summit. Continuing, the trail, now only a short distance from the real summit, reaches a six foot dropoff and another short descent before it begins its final ascent to a large rock hogback which climbs up to the open summit and a junction with the unmarked **Larry Dean Trail (1.8 m.).**

SUMMARY: Vt. 100 to summit, 1.8 m.; 1320 ft. ascent; 1½ hr. (Rev. 1 hr.).

Larry Dean Trail

Named for a veteran Scouter and Green Mountain Club member, the trail leaves the Mount Norris Trail at an unmarked junction in a large clearing, 0.7 m. from Vt. 100.

From the junction (0.0 m.), the trail continues through the clearing beside the brook, ignores a blue-blazed trail to the left (0.1 m.), and follows an old woods road, which is wet in places, on easy grades. Soon after crossing a brook and passing a woods road to the right (0.6 m.), the trail turns to the right into the woods, briefly follows the woods road, and then returns to the woods (0.7 m.). After ascending into a hollow and crossing a small stream (1.0 m.), the trail begins a steady winding climb past occasional views of Jay Peak and Belvidere Mt. to the summit and a junction with the **Mount Norris Trail (1.5 m.).**

SUMMARY: Vt. 100 to summit, 2.2 m.; 1320 ft. ascent; 1¾ hr. (Rev. 1¼ hr.).

Stone Mountain

Located in the town of Guildhall (USGS Guildhall), the heavily wooded summit (elev. 2753) no longer offers any views, since the old fire tower has been removed. There is still a trail to the summit, which follows logging roads for much of its length.

The trail begins on the Guildhall-Granby road, 3.7 m. west of Vt. 102 between US 2 and Guildhall village, and 7.2 m. east of Gallup Mills. Parking is available in a small clearing on the south side of the road.

From the road (0.0 m.), the trail follows a logging road south and ascends gradually. After passing several skid roads that branch off, the logging road bears east and reaches a small clearing (1.0 m.). Going straight through the clearing, the trail follows an old logging road and turns right (1.2 m.), leaving the road. It climbs steeply to a spring (1.6 m.), and continues to the old fire tower clearing on the summit (1.7 m.). From the ledges on the east and south there are very limited views through the trees.

BURKE MOUNTAIN

Located in East Burke (USGS Burke), Burke Mountain (elev. 3267) has a ski area, private campground, toll road, and communications facilities on its west slopes and summit. The mountain's hiking trails provide excellent views of the surrounding area. In addition to the trails described, there are a number of cross-country ski trails in the area.

Toll Road

About 3 m. long, this paved road leading to a parking area a short distance below the summit was constructed by the CCC. The road branches to the left from the access road leading to the Burke Mt. Ski Area, 2.2 m. from Vt. 114 at East Burke and 0.5 m. below the base lodge parking area. A toll is charged for vehicles, but hikers may use the road without charge.

From the upper parking area, there are local trails to the summit and to West Peak.

CCC Road

Blazed with blue diamonds, this multi-use trail leaves the Toll Road 0.6 m. above the ski area access road. Ascending to the south on easy grades, the CCC Road crosses several ski trails and open slopes, which offer good views to the west, and then continues in the woods to the height of land (1.5 m.). Here the **West Peak Trail** departs on the left.

From the height of land, the CCC Road descends easily to the southeast in the shallow notch between Burke Mt. and Kirby Mt. Soon after passing a leanto on the right (2.1 m.), the trail reaches a junction with a privately maintained snowmobile trail (orange diamonds), which leaves on the right (2.2 m.), and heads westerly for about 1¼ m. to a public road between North Kirby and East Burke. Beyond the junction, the CCC Road descends on easy grades past the state forest boundary to a woods road junction (3.2 m.).

Straight ahead from the junction, an old road descends on easy grades for about 1¼ m. to the beginning of a public road which leads south for about 3½ m. to the Victory—Granby Road, about 1 m. south of the Mitchell's Landing parking area.

SUMMARY: Toll Road to state forest boundary, 3.2 m.; 450 ft. ascent; 1¾ hr. (Rev. 2 hr.).

West Peak Trail

For the most part following the former Darling Trail, this blue-blazed trail leaves the **CCC Road** at its highest point, 1.5 m. south of the Burke Mt. Toll Road. From the junction (0.0 m.), the trail rises a short distance to a log leanto and then climbs steadily through the woods. After passing a limited view to the west (0.6 m.), the trail follows circuitous routing on easy grades to an open rock area (0.8 m.), where there are excellent views of the Passumpsic valley, the Lake Willoughby area, and the northern Green Mountains.

Soon returning to the woods, the trail passes a log leanto on the **west peak** (elev. 3100 ft.) of **Burke Mt. (0.9 m.)**, just beyond which there is a good view to the south. The trail then follows easy grades past a spur to a shelter and picnic area (1.1 m.) to a parking area and upper ski left station at the end of the **Toll Road (1.2 m.)**.

Beyond the parking area, the unblazed but obvious **Profile Trail** follows easy grades through the woods for 0.2 m. to a junction, where there is a choice of routes to the summit of Burke Mt. The somewhat longer and more interesting route to the right soon passes under an overhanging rock ledge and then follows a narrow canyon to the summit (elev. 3267 ft.) and the fire tower (0.4 m.).

SUMMARY: CCC Road to main summit, 1.6 m.; 960 ft. ascent; 1¼ hr. (Rev. ¾ hr.).

Maidstone State Park

Located at the southern end of Maidstone Lake (USGS Guildhall), Maidstone State Park (campgrounds, picnic area, swimming) is reached by following Vt. 102 south about 5 m. from Bloomfield and then following a gravel road southwest for another 5 m. The park has nature trails as well as a nature center. Obtain detailed information at the park.

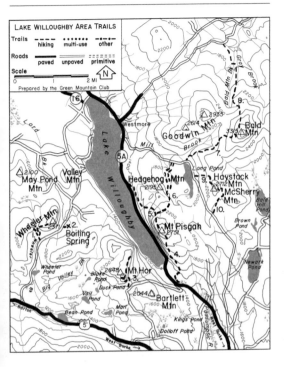

LAKE WILLOUGHBY AREA

Long acclaimed as one of the most scenic areas in Vermont, Lake Willoughby (USGS Lyndonville, Memphremagog) has become the center of an extensive trail system in recent years. Under the auspices of the Westmore Association, old trails have been restored and new trails built to reach major area peaks. Trail numbers used in the descriptions correspond to those on the area map.

Wheeler Mountain (1)

Despite its relatively low elevation (2371 ft.), Wheeler Mt. (see USGS Lyndonville) offers some of the finest and most varied views in the Lake Willoughby area. A white-blazed trail to the summit and Eagle Cliff is maintained by the Trail Committee of the Westmore Association.

The trail begins on the Wheeler Mountain Road, which leaves the north side of US 5, 8.3 m. north of Vt. 5A in West Burke and 5.0 m. south of Vt. 16 in Barton. From the highway this unpaved road climbs steadily past Wheeler Pond (1.0 m.) to the trailhead and parking area on the left, opposite the second of two houses (1.9 m.).

From the parking area (0.0 m.), the trail follows an old road northerly through an overgrown field to a junction, where alternate routing begins (0.1 m.). To the right, a shorter and more difficult red-blazed route quickly enters the woods and soon begins a steep and winding climb over the rocks, where there are views of Norris Mt. and Wheeler Pond, to rejoin the main trail 0.3 m. from the junction. The main trail takes the left fork and follows less demanding routing.

From the junction, the main trail soon enters the woods and ascends easily for some distance before beginning a short but stiff climb (0.4 m.). Soon after turning sharply to the right, the trail continues on easier grades past a view of Wheeler Pond (0.5 m.) to an open rock area, where the red alternate route rejoins the main trail (0.7 m.). A few feet beyond, a small sign indicates an unblazed spur to the left, which ascends about 100 ft. to a view of the Jay Peak.

From the spur junction, the trail winds through spruce and birches for some distance and then returns to open rock (0.9 m.). Remaining well away from the cliffs comprising the southeast face of the mountain, the trail climbs steadily in the open past ever widening views of Lake Willoughby, Mt. Pisgah, Burke Mt., and Bald Mt. to an impressive vantage point (1.1 m.) where the panorama also includes views of Jay Peak, Mt. Mansfield, and many other peaks in the Green Mountain range.

Beyond the lookout, the trail climbs gradually in the open for some distance and then enters the woods near the summit (1.2 m.) and descends through spruce and balsams to the end of the trail at **Eagle Cliff (1.3 m.).** Here there is an especially grand view of Lake Willoughby, with the open fields in the foreground providing an interesting contrast to the sheer cliffs of Mt. Pisgah and the numerous mountains in the background.

   SUMMARY: Parking area to Eagle Cliff via white main trail, 1.3 m.; Eagle Cliff via red alternate route, 1.1 m.; 690 ft. ascent; 1 hr. (Rev. ¾ hr.).

Boiling Spring (2)

   From a parking area on the Wheeler Mountain Road, 0.6 m. north of the Wheeler Mountain trailhead, a white-blazed trail, maintained by the Trail Committee of the Westmore Association, trends easterly through the woods with little change in elevation for 0.1 m. to a shallow sag. Here **Boiling Spring** discharges enough water to create a large pool and a swift running brook of remarkable size.

Mt. Hor (3)

   Forming the west side of the Lake Willoughby gateway, Mt. Hor (see USGS Lyndonville) is notable for the sheer cliffs which rise more than a thousand feet above the water. A blue-blazed trail with two branches, built and maintained by the Trail Committee of the Westmore Association, provides access to two lookouts on the east and a third vantage point just west of the wooded summit.
   The trail begins on the CCC Road, 1.8 m. west of its junction with Vt. 5A. The CCC Road leaves Vt. 5A at a parking area opposite the beginning of the South Trail to Mt. Pisgah, 4.2 m. south of the Millbrook Store in Westmore and 5.7 m. north of US 5 in West Burke. From US 5, 8.3 m. south of its junction with Vt. 16 South in Barton, it is 2.5 m. to the trail via the CCC Road. Parking is available 200 ft. east of the trailhead.
   From the CCC Road (0.0 m.), the trail to Mt. Hor ascends steadily, for the most part, on an old woods road. Turning sharply to the left when the road peters out (0.4 m.), the trail climbs moderately at first and then quite steeply past a piped spring (0.6 m.) to a junction and trail register just below the summit ridge (0.7 m.).
   From the junction, the **west branch** of the trail turns to the left. After ascending steadily for some distance, it continues on easy grades to a point just below the summit and then descends a short distance to **Summit Lookout (1.0 m.).** In the foreground can be seen ten small ponds, among them Bean, Wheeler, Blake, Duck, Vail, and Marl. Burke Mt. is

visible on the left. Hazens Notch and several of the northern Green Mountain peaks lie to the northwest.

From the junction (0.7 m.), the **east branch** turns to the right and continues just below ridgeline with only minor changes in elevation to a spur on the right, which descends for about 150 ft. to Willoughby or **East Lookout (1.3 m.)**, some 1200 ft. directly above the lake and directly opposite the Mt. Pisgah cliffs.

From the East Lookout spur, the recently extended trail descends to the **North Lookout (1.4 m.)**. Here there is a sweeping view of the north end of Lake Willoughby, beyond which can be seen the lower end of Lake Memphremagog and several peaks along the Vermont—Quebec border. Bald Mt. lies to the left of Mt. Pisgah.

SUMMARY: CCC Road to Summit Lookout, 1.0 m.; 700 ft. ascent; ¾ hr. (Rev. ½ hr.). CCC Road to North Lookout, 1.4 m.; 550 ft. ascent; 1 hr. (Rev. ¾ hr.).

EMERGENCIES
In case of an emergency on the trail, contact the Vermont State Police.

Sending in your reports of trail conditions will help the GMC keep this guide book up to date, and keep hikers advised of hiking conditions. Please fill out and mail the form in the back of this book.

Mount Pisgah

Forming the east side of the classic Lake Willoughby profile, Mt. Pisgah (see USGS Lyndonville) has long been popular with hikers. From the sheer cliffs which rise more than a thousand feet above the lake, there are numerous vantage points from which to enjoy the fine local and distant views. Two blue-blazed trails from Vt. 5A, both maintained by the Trail Committee of the Westmore Association, form a continuous route over the mountain. Completion of the loop, however, requires a scenic three mile walk along the highway. A third Westmore Association trail provides indirect routing to the summit from Long Pond.

The trails near the cliffs may be closed by the State of Vermont during the summer if peregrine falcons are nesting in the area.

South Trail (4)

This trail begins on the east side of Vt. 5A, opposite a state parking area and the beginning of the CCC Road, 5.8 m. south of the junction of Routes 16 and 5A at the north end of Lake Willoughby and 5.8 m. north of the junction of US 5 and Vt. 5A in West Burke.

From the highway (0.0 m.), the trail descends an embankment and quickly reaches a junction with the **Willoughby Nature Trail.** Constructed in 1977 by the Youth Conservation Corps, this self-guiding trail leads south past several stations for 0.1 m. to the base of a beaver dam.

From the nature trail spur, the South Trail crosses a muddy area on a newly constructed bridge and then crosses Swampy's Pond, considerably swollen by the beaver dam, on another bridge (0.1 m.). Turning to the left, the trail then follows a hogback to a woods road junction (0.2 m.). Here the trail turns to the right and ascends for some distance through rocky terrain before again turning sharply to the left (0.4 m.) and beginning a stiff climb. Soon after negotiating a switchback (0.5 m.), the trail continues on much easier grades past three lookouts on the left to **Pulpit Rock (0.9 m.).** Here there is an impressive view of Lake Willoughby, some 550 feet directly below, and of Mt. Hor.

From Pulpit Rock, the trail bears to the right and soon begins a steady climb and eventually reaches an open area (1.7 m.), where there are views to the south of the White Mountains, Victory Basin, Newark Pond, Burke Mt., and some of the Green Mountains. From the open area, the trail continues a short distance to the summit and the upper end of the **North Trail (5) (1.7 m.).**

From the summit, a short spur leads to an easterly vista. Via the North Trail, it is 0.3 m. to two lookouts providing outstanding views of Lake Willoughby, Lake Memphremagog, and the Green Mountains. It is 2.2 m. to Vt. 5A, 3.0 m. north of the beginning of the South Trail.

SUMMARY: Highway to summit, 1.7 m.; 1450 ft. ascent; 1¾ hr. (Rev. 1 hr.).

North Trail (5)

The trail begins on the east side of Vt. 5A, 3.0 m. south of the junction of Vt. 16 near the north end of Lake Willoughby and 3.0 m. north of the beginning of the South Trail. Limited parking is available near the trailhead.

From the highway (0.0 m.), the trail ascends a steep bank and soon enters the woods, following old woods roads on easy grades. After crossing two brooks (0.6 m. and 0.8 m.), the trail follows somewhat steeper grades to a third brook crossing, the last certain water on the trail (1.0 m.). Beyond the third brook crossing, the trail turns sharply to the left and climbs fairly steeply on an old road. Soon turning to the right off the road (1.2 m.), the trail climbs steeply on rough footing to a junction with a white-blazed trail (6), which departs on the left for Long Pond (1.5 m.).

From the junction, the trail climbs somewhat less steeply over rough ground to the first of two spur trails, located about 150 ft. apart (1.9 m.). The lower spur leads about 350 ft. northwest to the **North Lookout,** while the upper spur leads west about 75 ft. to the **West Lookout.** Although the views are about the same from each vantage point, the differences in elevation and angle of view provide somewhat different perspectives.

From the Upper Lookout, some 1400 feet directly above the lake and the highway, the views include Mt. Hor, Wheeler Mt., and other local peaks; Lake Memphremagog. Owl's Head, Bear Mt. and other Quebec summits to the north; many of the Green Mountain peaks from Jay Peak south to Camel's Hump; and Burke Mt. and a number of New Hampshire peaks to the south, including Mt. Moosilauke.

From the lookout spurs, the trail continues to the summit of Mt. Pisgah and the north end of the **South Trail (4) (2.2 m.).** A short distance beyond, an open area offers views to the south. From the summit, via the South Trail, it is 1.7 m. to Vt. 5A, 3.0 m. south of the beginning of the North Trail.

SUMMARY: Highway to summit, 2.2 m.; 1530 ft. ascent; 2 hr. (Rev. 1¼ hr.).

Long Pond-Mt. Pisgah Trail (6)

Maintained by the Trail Committee of the Westmore Association, this white-blazed trail provides a connecting link between the Mt. Pisgah trails and the routes to Bald Mt. and Haystack Mt.

The northern terminus of the trail is off Long Pond Rd. From the Millbrook Store on Vt. 5A, go east (uphill) for 1.8 m. Turn right on onto a logging road and park at the gate.

From the gate (0.0 m.), the trail follows the logging road to a fork (1.2 m.). Taking a right, the trail then goes over a low ridge and crosses a small stream in a sag (1.5 m.). It climbs to an old woods road, where it turns to the right (1.6 m.). After ascending easily for some distance, the trail climbs somewhat more steeply to a junction with the **North Trail (5)** to Mt. Pisgah **(2.0 m.)**. From this point, it is 0.7 m. to the summit of Mt. Pisgah and 1.5 m. downhill to Vt. 5A.

SUMMARY: Long Pond Road to North Trail, 2.0 m.; 350 ft. ascent; 1¼ hr. (Rev. 1 hr.).

SPRING HIKING DISCOURAGED

The Green Mountain Club discourages hiking during the spring mud season, usually from mid-April to the end of May. Snow lingering at the higher elevations creates very wet and muddy conditions. Hiker's boots do much more damage to wet and muddy trails than when the trails are dry and more stable.

Bald Mountain

Sometimes referred to as Westmore Mt., Bald Mt. (see USGS Island Pond) has a summit clearing, from which there are good local views to the south and east, and an abandoned fire tower. The extensive views from the tower include Lake Willoughby, various local peaks, and much of the Green Mountain range to the west; Lake Seymour, Lake Memphremagog, and several Quebec mountains to the north and northwest; Island Pond, Percy Peaks, the Columbia Range, and northern White Mountain peaks to the east; and Burke Mt., Umpire Mt., and the Presidentials to the south.

There are two trails to the summit. The abandoned but still well used Lookout's Trail ascends from the north, and the Westmore Association's trail starts at Long Pond from the southwest.

Long Pond-Bald Mountain Trail (7)

Maintained by the Trail Committee of the Westmore Association, this yellow-glazed trail begins about 350 ft. east of the Long Pond public access area, which is reached by following a public road 2.0 m. east from the Millbrook Store on Vt. 5A in Westmore. Ample parking is available at the Long Pond access area.

From the Long Pond Road, a short distance above the access area (0.0 m.), the trail enters a woods road on the left. For the most part following old roads in a northeasterly direction, the trail ascends on easy to moderate grades around the shoulder of a nameless mountain (elev. 2610 ft.) and eventually crosses a small stream in a sag (1.0 m.). Quickly crossing three more very small streams, the trail continues to a larger brook, where it turns sharply to the right after crossing it (1.3 m.).

Beyond the brook crossing, the trail ascends steadily for some distance and then continues on easier grades to an old woods road junction (1.5 m.). Here the trail turns sharply to the right and begins an increasingly steep climb in an easterly direction. After swinging around a large rock outcrop and limited views to the southwest (1.8 m.), the trail continues a steady winding ascent for some distance before bearing to the left (2.0 m.) and continuing on easy grades to the summit (2.1 m.).

SUMMARY: Long Pond Road to summit, 2.1 m.; 1450 ft. ascent; 1¾ hr. (Rev. 1 hr.).

Lookout's Trail (8)

Although no longer formally maintained, this unblazed and unsigned route still receives considerable use and is easily followed.

The trail is reached via secondary roads leading east from the white church on Vt. 5A in Westmore, 1.0 m. south of the junction of Vt. 16 and about 11 miles north of US 5 in West Burke. From the highway and the church (0.0 m.), follow the paved road uphill to the east, take a fork to the right (0.5 m.), and continue to the next junction (2.0 m.), where a large glacial boulder is visible in the field to the left. Turn right, continue past a fork to the right (2.7 m.), and descend to a fork, where an old road goes to the right (3.7 m.). While this abandoned road may be passable, with caution, it is recommended that hiking start at this junction. Limited parking is available in the vicinity.

From the road junction (0.0 m.), the trail ascends in a southerly direction along the old road to a fork and an old trail arrow (0.6 m.). Here the trail turns to the left, fords **Bald Mountain Brook,** and continues along the old road to the upper end of a large overgrown field (0.8 m.). Bearing to the right, the trail soon begins an easy climb through pleasant hardwoods and eventually reaches a small piped spring on the left, the last certain source of water on the trail (2.0 m.). Beyond the spring, the grade increases and soon becomes quite steep. After passing views to the north of Echo Lake and Lake Seymour (2.6 m.), the trail continues on easier grades to the summit and the fire tower (2.8 m.).

SUMMARY: Public road to summit, 2.8 m.; 1690 ft. ascent; 2¼ hr. (Rev. 1½ hr.).

Haystack Mountain

Just below the heavily wooded summit of the aptly named mountain (see USGS Lyndonville) are three lookouts providing excellent views to the west, south, and east. There are two trails to the summit, both established and maintained by the Trail Committee of the Westmore Association.

North Trail (9)

This orange-blazed trail, the steeper of the two routes, begins at the entrance to a small clearing on the Long Pond Road, 2.6 m. east and south of Vt. 5A at the Millbrook Store in Westmore and 0.6 m. above the Long Pond public access area. Parking space is very limited, and care should be taken not to obstruct the narrow public road.

From the road (0.0 m.), the trail quickly passes through the clearing with its overgrown cellar hole and climbs steadily in an easterly direction on an old woods road. Eventually assuming a southerly direction (0.4 m.), the trail continues for some distance on easier grades before beginning (0.7 m.) a moderately steep climb past views of Bald Mt. and Long Pond (0.8 m.) to a junction (1.0 m.). To the left, it is about 75 ft. to the summit, which is marked by a large cairn. To the right, a spur descends easily for about 150 ft. to **West Lookout**, where there are views of Long Pond, Lake Willoughby, Wheeler Mt. and Jay Peak.

From the summit, the **South Trail** descends 0.1 m. to the **East Lookout** and 0.2 m. to the **South Lookout**.

SUMMARY: Road to summit, 1.0 m.; 875 ft. ascent; 1 hr. (Rev. ½ hr.).

South Trail (10)

Blazed yellow, this trail begins at the Long Pond Road, 3.8 m. east and south of Vt. 5A at the Millbrook Store in Westmore, 1.8 m. above the Long Pond public access area, and 1.2 m. south of the North Trail. Ample parking is available at the trailhead.

From the road (0.0 m.), the trail ascends gradually in a northeasterly direction on an old road to a junction in a large overgrown clearing (0.6 m.). Here the trail turns to the left, passes to the right of an old camp, and continues on easy grades through a series of small brushy clearings before entering the woods. Soon turning sharply to the left

(0.8 m.), the trail then begins a steep and winding ascent around the rocks to a junction (0.9 m.). Here a spur leads about 125 ft. left to the **South Lookout,** where there are views of Burke Mt. and Newark Pond.

From the South Lookout spur, the trail ascends to the **East Lookout** (1.0 m.), where there are views of Bald Mt., Bald Hill Pond, East Haven Mt., and various White Mountain peaks. From the East Lookout, the trail continues to a large cairn marking the summit of **Haystack Mt. (1.1 m.).** A short distance beyond, the trail reaches a junction with the **North Trail,** which leaves to the right. Continuing straight ahead for about 150 ft., the trail ends at the **West Lookout.**

SUMMARY: Road to summit and West Lookout, 1.1 m.; 525 ft. ascent; ¾ hr. (Rev. ½ hr.).

Brighton State Park

Located on the south shore of Island Pond and the west shore of Spectacle Pond, Brighton State Park (campground, picnic area) is reached by following a paved town road south for about ¾ m. from Vt. 105, about 2 m. east of the village of Island Pond.

Three blue-blazed trails, in part used as a self-guiding nature trail, are located along or near the shore of **Spectacle Pond** and are reached from the camping area. A nature trail guide and map of the approximately 1½ m. system is available at the park.

When parking vehicles at trailheads and road junctions, hikers should take special care to avoid obstructing traffic or blocking access to homes, farms, or woodlots. Vandalism can be a problem at some trailhead parking areas, and it may be wiser to leave your car in town, especially if you will be out overnight.

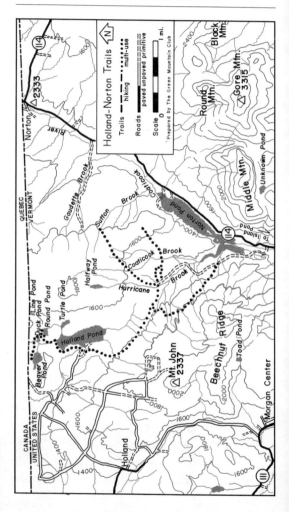

BILL SLADYK WILDLIFE MANAGEMENT AREA

Administered by the Vermont Department of Fish and Wildlife, the Bill Sladyk WMA consists of about 10,000 acres in the towns of Holland, Norton, Warren's Gore, and Warner's Grant (see USGS Island Pond). Although there are no officially marked or maintained hiking trails, most of the area is restricted to travel by foot or snowmobile.

In addition to the many miles of old woods roads, there are several miles of wildlife habitat management access roads and numerous privately maintained snowmobile trails, some of which have signs and orange diamond markers at junction points. The guide book map shows only a few of the major trails, some of which continue across private lands, and the USGS Island Pond map should be consulted for more serious exploration. Because this is big country with few conspicuous landmarks, the prospective hiker should be especially observant and be familiar with the use of map and compass. This being state land, fires and overnight camping are prohibited by law.

Round Pond and Beaver Pond

Located in the northwest corner of the WMA, these primitive natural ponds are reached from the west side of Holland Pond. From the village of Holland, located on a gravel road about 5 m. north of Vt. 111 at Morgan Center, continue north for about 3 m. to a junction. Turn right and continue easterly about 2½ m. to a fork, then bear left and continue to the shore of Holland Pond. A short distance to the north is a gate and a parking area.

From the gate, an old road leads north, following the west and north shores of **Holland Pond.** Just beyond a brook crossing (about ¾ m.), the trail swings to the north at an old junction and continues to another junction (about 1¼ m.) near the north shore of **Round Pond.** Taking the left fork, the trail soon swings around tiny **Duck Pond** and continues westerly to the northeast corner of **Beaver Pond** (about 2 m.).

SUMMARY: Norton Pond gate to Beaver Pond, about 2 m.; 150 ft. ascent; 1 hr. (Rev. 1 hr.).

DIRECTORY OF TRAIL ORGANIZATIONS

APPALACHIAN TRAIL CONFERENCE, P.O. Box 807, Harpers Ferry, WV 25425

Coordinates the work of the many organizations and individuals who maintain the Appalachian Trail from Maine to Georgia. Publishes *Guide to the Appalachian Trail in New Hampshire and Vermont* (1988) and other guide books. Free publications list.

ASCUTNEY TRAILS ASSOCIATION, 32 Elm St., Windsor, VT 05089

Maintains trails and shelters on Mt. Ascutney and schedules frequent outings. Publishes *Guide to the Trails of Ascutney Mountain.*

CATAMOUNT TRAIL ASSOCIATION, P.O. Box 897, Burlington, VT 05402

Maintains the Catamount Trail, a cross-country ski trail linking the trail networks of many ski touring centers between Massachusetts and Canada. Publishes *Catamount Trail Ski Map of Vermont.*

CONSERVATION SOCIETY OF SOUTHERN VERMONT, RR 1, Newfane, VT 05345

Maintains trails and operates Summer Conservation School in the 3000 acre West River Valley Greenway in Jamaica and South Londonderry. Publishes *A Trail Guide to the West River Valley Greenway.* Facilities open for use by organizations and private parties by arrangement with the Vermont Dept. of Forests, Parks, and Recreation in Waterbury.

GREEN MOUNTAIN NATIONAL FOREST, Forest Supervisor, P.O. Box 519, Rutland, VT 05701

Maintains portions of the Long Trail system, various other trails, and several recreation areas including campgrounds and picnic areas. Forest map, day hiking guides and other publications are available. District Ranger offices are located in Manchester, Middlebury, and Rochester.

MERCK FOREST, Route 315, Rupert, VT 05768

Over 2600 acres devoted to education, conservation, and recreation. Publishes free trail map of 26 mile trail system. Group camping available by advance arrangement.

NEW ENGLAND TRAIL CONFERENCE, 33 Knollwood Dr., East Longmeadow, MA 01028

A clearing house for information about the trails and shelters maintained by many organizations and public agencies in New England. Annual meeting each spring brings together representatives of member organizations and is open to all interested persons. Answers trail inquiries. Publishes *Hiking Trails of New England*, a sketch map and trail bibliography.

TACONIC HIKING CLUB OF TROY, NEW YORK, 810 Church Street Ext., Troy, NY 12180

Maintains Taconic Crest Trail between North Pownal, Vt. and Berry Pond, Ma. Publishes *Taconic Crest Trail Guide*.

VERMONT DEPARTMENT OF FORESTS, PARKS, AND RECREATION, 103 South Main St., Waterbury, VT 05676

Part of the Agency of Environmental Conservation, the department maintains hiking and multi-use trails, campgrounds, picnic areas, and other recreational facilities in various state parks and forests. Publishes *Vermont State Parks and Forest Recreation Areas* and *Vermont Guide to Primitive Camping on State Lands*, available free at most information centers and state parks. Free trail maps are available at many parks or from agency regional offices in Essex Junction, Barre, St. Johnsbury, Pittsford, and North Springfield.

WESTMORE ASSOCIATION TRAIL COMMITTEE, c/o Mrs. Arthur Poisson, RFD 1, Barton, VT 05822

Maintains trails in the Lake Willoughby area. Publishes free map and guide of area trails.

WILLIAMS OUTING CLUB, Williams College, Williamstown, MA 01267

Maintains trails in southwest Vermont and northwest Massachusetts.

WOODSTOCK PARK COMMISSION, Woodstock, VT 05091

Maintains local trails in Faulkner and Billings Parks. Free trail map available.

TOPOGRAPHIC MAPS

The *Index to Topographic Maps of New Hampshire and Vermont* shows current coverage of maps in the 7½ and 15 minute series. The index and a pamphlet describing topographic maps are available without charge from the Branch of Distribution, U.S. Geological Survey, 1200 South Eads St., Arlington, VA 22202. Maps are available locally in many outdoor and office supply stores.

INDEX

This index is limited to the trails, mountains, bodies of water, and other significant landmarks described or mentioned in the individual trail descriptions. Only the most important page references are given.

GMC PUBLICATIONS

The Green Mountain Club welcomes inquiries about hiking and backpacking in Vermont, and about Trail conditions and planning. For more information, or to order the Club publications and slide shows described below, write or call:

> The Green Mountain Club, Inc.
> P.O. Box 889
> Montpelier, VT. 05602
>
> (802) 223-3463

Guide Book

Guide Book of the Long Trail - (23rd edition, 1989) Pocket sized guide with 16 color topographical maps. Complete description of the Long Trail, its side trails and shelters; hiking suggestions and helpful hints.

Trail Maps

End to End: Topographic Maps of Vermont's Long Trail - (1988) A set of 21 color topographical maps of the Long Trail printed on weather resistant paper; designed to be used in conjunction with the *Guide Book of the Long Trail*.

Camel's Hump - (1985) Color, fold-out topographical map of the Camel's Hump area; weather resistant, with trail mileages, overnight facilities, trail heads, regulations, and other information.

Mt. Mansfield - (1987) Color, fold-out topographical map of the Mt. Mansfield area; weather resistant, with trail mileages, overnight facilities, trail heads, regulations, and other information.

Mt. Mansfield Booklet

Tundra Trail - A Self-Guiding Walk: Life, Man and the Ecosystem on Top of Mt. Mansfield, Vermont - This 12 page booklet with illustrations describes a natural history hike along the Long Trail on the summit ridgeline of Mt. Mansfield.

GMC History

Green Mountain Adventure, Vermont's Long Trail - (1st edition, 1985) An illustrated history of the Green Mountain Club by Jane & Will Curtis and Frank Lieberman. Ninety-six pages of rare black-and-white photographs and anecdotes of the Club's first 75 years.

Pamphlets

"The Long Trail: A Footpath in the Wilderness" - Pamphlet with information and suggestions on hiking the Long Trail. Free with Self-Addressed Stamped Envelope (SASE).

"Day Hiker's Vermont Sampler" - Pamphlet with map of Vermont and descriptions of several hikes throughout the state; hiking tips and suggestions. Free with SASE.

"Winter Trail Use in the Green Mountains" - Pamphlet containing basic information about using the Long Trail system in winter. Free with SASE.

Slide Shows

Mt. Mansfield - Capstone of Vermont - Color slides and sound narration describes Vermont's highest mountain and its special characteristics, and tells how visitors can help preserve the mountain while they hike it safely. Produced by Louis Borie. 25 minutes.

Beyond the Limit of Trees: New England's Alpine Areas - Color slides and narration provide a close-up look at these unusual natural areas in Vermont, New Hampshire and Maine; with information about their origins and characteristics, the hazards facing them, and the efforts to protect and preserve them. Produced by Peter Zika. 20 minutes.

A fact sheet containing details and rental information for the slide shows is available from the GMC office.

AN INVITATION
TO JOIN THE
GREEN MOUNTAIN CLUB

P.O. Box 889
Montpelier, Vermont 05602

Individuals and organizations who wish to support the Long Trail System may join the Club as either AT-LARGE or SECTION members. (See Reverse Side)

_____
Name(s)

_____
Street

_____
City   State   Zip

Telephone Number _____

I enclose $_____ annual dues for membership in the Green Mountain Club.

Please check **ONLY ONE:**

☐ AT-LARGE

☐ SECTION: _____

●

SECTION MEMBERSHIP

GMC Sections are semi-autonomous local "chapters" which conduct hikes and other activities, and maintain a portion of the Long Trail System. They are as follows:

Bennington	VT
Brattleboro	VT
Bread Loaf	Middlebury, VT
Burlington	VT
Connecticut	CT
Killington	Rutland, VT
Laraway	Northwestern VT
Manchester	VT
Montpelier	VT
*New York	NY, NJ
Ottauquechee	Woodstock, VT
Pioneer Valley	Western MA
Sterling	Morrisville, VT
Worcester	Eastern MA

*Dues schedule above is for provisional New York Section membership.

AT-LARGE MEMBERSHIP

Individuals who wish to support the work of the Club but not interested in joining a Section may join as At-Large members.

MEMBERSHIP DUES SCHEDULE

☐ Individual..$ 18.00
☐ Spouse of Member ....$ 5.00
☐ Student Member (Under 23)..................$ 12.00
☐ Junior Member (Under 18)....................$ 8.00
☐ Junior Family Member.........................$ 1.50
☐ Organizations....................................$ 30.00
☐ Institutional......................................$100.00
☐ Life Membership................................$300.00

HAVE YOU SPOTTED A PROBLEM ON THE TRAIL?

Sending in your reports of trail conditions will help maintainers establish priorities for maintenance and improvements on the 150 trails in this guide. Please fill out this form and mail it to the Green Mountain Club, P.O. Box 889, Montpelier, VT 05602.

TRAIL(S): _____

_____

_____

LOCATION(S): _____

_____

_____

PROBLEM(S): _____

_____

_____

_____

_____

_____

May a trail maintainer contact you for followup information if needed?

Name: _____

Address: _____

_____

Phone: _____

Date: _____

THANK YOU!